The Marketing Audit

The Marketing Series is one of the most comprehensive collections of books in marketing and sales available from the UK today.

Published by Butterworth-Heinemann on behalf of the Chartered Institute of Marketing, the series is divided into three distinct groups: *Student* (fulfilling the needs of those taking the Institute's certificate and diploma qualifications); *Professional Development* (for those on formal or self-study vocational training programmes); and *Practitioner* (presented in a more informal, motivating and highly practical manner for the busy marketer).

STUDENT | PROFESSIONAL DEVELOPMENT | PRACTITIONER

Formed in 1911, the Chartered Institute of Marketing is now the largest professional marketing management body in Europe with over 24,000 members and 28,000 students located worldwide. Its primary objectives are focused on the development of awareness and understanding of marketing throughout UK industry and commerce and on the raising of standards of professionalism in the education, training and practice of this key business discipline.

The Marketing Audit

Translating marketing theory into practice

Malcolm H. B. McDonald

**Written in association
with John W. Leppard**

Butterworth-Heinemann Ltd
Linacre House, Jordan Hill, Oxford OX2 8DP

  A member of the Reed Elsevier plc group

OXFORD   LONDON   BOSTON   MUNICH
NEW DELHI   SINGAPORE   SYDNEY   TOKYO
TORONTO   WELLINGTON

First published 1991
Reprinted 1993
Paperback edition 1993
Reprinted 1994

© Malcolm H. B. McDonald 1991

British Library Cataloguing in Publication Data
McDonald, Malcolm H. B.
    The marketing audit: Translating marketing theory
    into practice.
    I. Title
    658.8

ISBN 0 7506 1706 3

Printed in England by Clays Ltd, St Ives plc

Contents

Preface

Marketing courses provide the necessary conceptual framework for marketers, just as engineering courses do for engineers, human resource programmes do for personnel managers, and so on. In the cut and thrust of the real world, however, problems do not come as neatly formed as theory would suggest, so 'students' of marketing need a bridge between the world of theory and the world of practice. That is the purpose of this book. The methods outlined here have been tried and tested by me over the years in thousands of organizations around the world. They are practical, and they work.

All the exercises in this book are designed to translate marketing theory into practice and to provide you with insights about your company, how it tackles various aspects of marketing, and how all these aspects can be integrated into a marketing plan. The exercises are *not* checklists, but actionable propositions. Some chapters have more exercises in them than others in order to reflect their relative importance in marketing planning. Also, a variety of different methods have been used, including, in Chapter 5, two short case studies.

The real objective of this book is to give you something which is the marketing equivalent of the road test to which cars are subjected. The application of the exercises will test out your organization's marketing 'roadworthiness'.

Although all the exercises in this book can be used independently of any other text, I do not recommend that readers should try using them without a solid foundation in marketing theory. Without such a solid conceptual basis, marketing skills are likely to be considerably blunted. Readers should first know what they are doing, and why, before they rush off and use this book. For this reason, it is recommended that the core text *Marketing Plans: how to prepare them; how to use them* (Butterworth Heinemann, 1989) should be carefully studied as a precursor to using the exercises in this book.

Professor Malcolm H. B. McDonald

Understanding the marketing process

The marketing concept

Providing goods or services for which there is a known customer demand, as opposed to selling what the company likes to produce. By focusing on customers and their wants the company is better positioned to make a profit. The company is then said to be market-led, or to have a 'market orientation'.

Try Exercise 1.1

Company capabilities

The company will not be equally good at all things. It will have strengths and weaknesses. The astute company tries to identify customer wants that best match its own strengths, be they its product range, relations with customers, technical expertise, flexibility, or whatever. Inevitably there is an element of compromise in the matching process, but successful companies strive to build on their strengths and reduce their weaknesses.

Try Exercise 1.2

The marketing environment

No business operates in a vacuum; it has an environment which not only contains all its existing and potential customers and its competitors, but many factors outside its control. Changes in the environment in terms of

- customer wants,
- fashions,
- technology,
- environmental concern,
- legislation,
- economic climate,
- competition, etc.,

present the company with both opportunities and threats. Keeping a finger on the pulse of the environment is essential for the successful company.

Try Exercise 1.3

Questions raised for the company

1 Is it different marketing a product or a service?
   The central ideas of marketing are universal.
2 What do customers want?
   They don't always know, but dialogue with them and intelligent research can help to answer this question.
3 Do we need to bother with marketing?
   Some companies are very successful by chance. They happen to be in the right place at the right time. Most other companies need to plan their marketing.

Try Exercise 1.4

4 Do we need a marketing department?
   Not necessarily. It will depend upon the size and complexity of the company's range of products and services. The higher the complexity, the more difficult it is to coordinate activities and achieve the 'matching' of a company to its customers.

Introduction

As you work through this book, you will find that some of the exercises are diagnostic and enable you to 'plot' where your company is. Some will help you to understand what might be happening to your company. Other exercises are more concerned with generating factual information about your company, its products, its markets or its planning processes. We find this combination of exercises not only provides you with insights and learning about many aspects of marketing planning, but it also helps you to assemble information which can contribute to a marketing plan for your company.

Whenever scoring and interpretation are required for an exercise, you will find the answers are provided at the end of each chapter.

This first chapter is designed to give you an opportunity to explore ways of looking at marketing. Exercise 1.1 enables you to make an assessment of your own beliefs about marketing. The remaining exercises can be applied to your organization.

Exercise 1.1 Marketing orientation

Below are a number of definitions of marketing that have appeared in books and journals over the last twenty or so years. Read through them carefully and note on a piece of paper the numbers of those which most accurately reflect your own views.

While there is no upper limit to the number of definitions you can choose, try, if you can, to limit your choice to a maximum of nine or ten definitions.

1   'The planning and execution of all aspects and activities of a product so as to exert optimum influence on the consumer, to result in maximum consumption at the optimum price and thereby producing the maximum long term profit.'

2   'Deciding what the customer wants; arranging to make it; distributing and selling it at a profit.'

3   'Marketing perceives consumption as a democratic process in which consumers have the right to select preferred candidates. They elect them by casting their money votes to those who supply the goods or services that satisfy their needs.'

4   'The planning, executing and evaluating of the external factors related to a company's profit objectives.'

5   'Adjusting the whole activity of a business to the needs of the customer or potential customer.'

6   '. . . marketing is concerned with the idea of satisfying the needs of customers by means of the product and a whole cluster of things associated with creating, delivering and finally, consuming it.'

7   'The total system of interacting business activities designed to plan, price, promote and distribute products and services to present and potential customers.'

8   '(Marketing is) the world of business seen from the point of view of its final result, that is from the customer's viewpoint. Concern and responsibility for marketing must therefore permeate all areas of the enterprise.'

9   'The activity that can keep in constant touch with an organization's consumers, read their needs and build a programme of communications to express the organization's purposes.'

10   'The management function which organizes and directs all those business activities involved in assessing and converting customer

purchasing power into effective demand for a specific product or service and moving the product or service to the final customer or user so as to achieve the profit target or other objectives set by the company.'

11 'The marketing concept emphasizes the vital importance to effective corporate planning and control, of monitoring both the environment in which the offering is made and the needs of the customers, in order that the process may operate as effectively as is humanly possible.'

12 'The organization and performance of those business activities that facilitate the exchange of goods and services between maker and user.'

13 'The process of: (1) Identifying customer needs, (2) Conceptualizing these needs in terms of the organization's capacity to produce, (3) Communicating that conceptualization to the appropriate locus of power in the organization, (4) Conceptualizing the consequent output in terms of the customer needs earlier identified, (5) Communicating that conceptualization to the customer.'

14 '(In a marketing company) all activities – from finance to production to marketing – should be geared to profitable consumer satisfaction.'

15 'The performance of those business activities that direct the flow of goods from producer to consumer or user.'

16 'The skill of selecting and fulfilling consumer wants so as to maximize the profitability per unit of capital employed in the enterprise.'

17 'The economic process by means of which goods and services are exchanged and their values determined in terms of money prices.'

18 'The performance of business activities that direct the flow of goods and services from producer to consumer in order to accomplish the firm's objectives.'

19 'Marketing is concerned with preventing the accumulation of non-moving stocks.'

20 'The activity that can keep in constant touch with an organization's consumers, read their needs and build a programme of communications to express the organization's purposes ... and means of satisfying them.'

SCORING FOR EXERCISE 1.1

You should have selected a number of definitions that you identify with. To work out your score, tick the boxes in the table below which equate to your chosen statements. Now add the number of ticks in each group and enter the total in the boxes at the end of each row.

Group A	1	2	4	7	10	12	15	17	18	19	
Group B	3	5	6	8	9	11	13	14	16	20	

For example, if you selected definitions 1, 3, 5, 6, 10 and 14, then 1 and 10 would score a total of 2 in Group A and 3, 5, 6 and 14 would score a total of 4 in Group B.

INTERPRETATION OF EXERCISE 1.1

If you study the various definitions, you will find that the essential difference between those in Group A and those in Group B is that *Group B definitions make an unambiguous reference about identifying and satisfying customer needs and building systems around this principle.* This is generally accepted as true marketing orientation, and is the stance taken throughout this book about marketing.

Group A definitions tend to focus far less on the customer (unless it is to *decide* what customers want, or to *exert influence* on the customer, i.e. to do things to the customer) and more on the company's own systems and profit motives. Thus Group A definitions could be described as being more traditional views about managing a business. Therefore the more Group B and the fewer Group A answers you have, then the higher your marketing orientation and the less at odds you should be with the ideas put forward in this book.

Please note that this is your personal orientation towards marketing and nothing to do with your company.

Exercise 1.2 Company capabilities and the matching process

1 Reflect on your company's recent history, say the last five years. Over that period, what would you say have been the key strengths that have carried the company to its present position?

   (a) Make a list of these below. *Note.* In a small company, among the strengths might be listed key people. Where this happens, expand on what the person actually brings to the organization, e.g. sales director – his/her contacts in the industry.
   (b) What would you say are the three main weaknesses at present?

   (i) --
   (ii) --
   (iii) --

2 Again, considering the last 5-year period, has the company got better at matching its strengths to customers and to its business environment, or worse?
   Often there are both positive and negative forces at work.
   (a) Make a note of the factors which led to improvements in the space below.

   (b) Make a note of the factors which led to a deterioration in the space below.

   At this stage you do not need to draw any specific conclusions from this exercise, although you will probably find it useful to return to this information as you progress through the book.

Exercise 1.3 The marketing environment

You will be asked to consider the marketing environment in more detail later. For now, think back over the last 5 years of the company's history and answer these questions:

1 Which were the three most significant *opportunities* in the environment which contributed to the company's success/present situation?

(a) .... (   )

(b) .... (   )

(c) .... (   )

Put a score against each factor listed, in the bracket, using a 1–10 scale (where 10 is extremely significant).

2 Which were the three most significant *threats* which operated against the company over this period and which inhibited its success?

(a) .... (   )

(b) .... (   )

(c) .... (   )

Again, score these threats on a 1–10 scale as above.

3 Reflect on what you have written above and consider whether or not these opportunities and threats are increasing or decreasing in significance, or if new ones are on the horizon. Make notes below. *Looking ahead for, say the next 3 years.*

Opportunities   →   ....

Threats   →   ....

Again, at this stage you do not need to draw any specific conclusions from this exercise, although you will probably find it useful to return to this information as you progress through the book.

Exercise 1.4   Marketing quiz*

Place a tick after each statement in the column which most accurately describes your company situation.

	Very true	True	Don't know	Untrue	Very untrue
1 (*a*) Our return on invested capital is satisfactory.					
(*b*) There is good evidence it will stay that way for the next 5 years.					
(*c*) Detailed analysis indicates that it is probably incapable of being materially improved.					
2 (*a*) Our market share is not declining.					
(*b*) This is a fact, based on objective evidence.					
(*c*) There is objective evidence that it will stay that way.					
3 (*a*) Our turnover is increasing.					
(*b*) At a rate faster than inflation.					
(*c*) But not at the expense of profitability.					
4 I know for sure that our sales organization is only allowed to push less profitable lines at the expense of more profitable ones if there are rational reasons for doing so.					
5 (*a*) I understand why the company has performed the way it has during the past 5 years.					
(*b*) I know (apart from hoping) where it is heading during the next 5 years.					
6 (*a*) I am wholly satisfied that we make what the market wants, not what we prefer to produce.					
(*b*) Our production, marketing, selling and advertising strategies are developed for the profitability of the company as a whole rather than for the gratification of any personal ambitions.					
(*c*) I am satisfied that we do not use short-term tactics which are injurious to our long-term interests.					
7 (*a*) I know that sales and profit forecasts presented by operating management are realistic.					
(*b*) I know they are as exacting as they can reasonably be.					
(*c*) If I or anyone insists that they are raised, it is because a higher level is attainable not just because a better-looking budget is required.					
8 (*a*) The detailed data generated internally are analysed to provide timely information about what is happening in the key areas of the business.					

* Adapted by Professor M. H. B. McDonald from a questionnaire devised by Harry Henry Associated in 1971.

	Very true	True	Don't know	Untrue	Very untrue
(b) Marketing research data which operating management acquires is synthesized into plain English and is actually needed and used in the key decision-making process.					
9 (a) We do not sell unprofitably to any customer.					
(b) We analyse our figures to be sure of this.					
(c) If we do, it is for rational reasons known to us all.					
10 Our marketing policies are based on market-centred opportunities which we have fully researched, not on vague hopes of doing better.					

*Adapted by Professor M.H.B. McDonald from a questionnaire devised by Harry Henry Associated in 1971.

Join up the ticks down the page and count how many are to the left of the *don't know* position, and how many are at the *don't know* position or to the right of it.

INTERPRETATION OF EXERCISE 1.4

If you have 11 or more answers in the *don't know* position or to the right of it, then the chances are that your company isn't very marketing-orientated. It needs to take a closer look at itself in the ways suggested by this book.

Scores between 12 and 20 to the left of the *don't know* position indicate an organization that appears to have reasonable control of many of the significant ingredients of commercial success. Nonetheless, there is clearly still room for improvement, and this book should be useful in bringing about such an improvement.

Scores above 20 to the left of the *don't know* position indicate an organization completely in command of the key success variables. Are you *certain* that this is a true reflection of your organization's situation? If you are, then the chances are that its marketing skills are already highly developed. However, this book will still be useful for newcomers to the marketing function who wish to learn about the marketing process, and it will certainly help to maintain your high standards.

2 The marketing planning process -- the main steps

What is marketing planning?

A logical sequence of events leading to the setting of marketing objectives and the formulation of plans for achieving them.

↓

The sequence is:

1 Set corporate objectives.
2 Conduct marketing audit.
3 Conduct SWOT analysis.
4 Make assumptions.
5 Set marketing objectives
6 Estimate expected results.
7 Identify alternative plans and mixes.
8 Establish programmes.
9 Measure and review progress.

Try Exercise 2.1

↓

The plan itself contains:

1 Mission statement*
2 Financial summary.
3 Market overview.
4 SWOT analysis.
5 Assumptions.
6 Marketing objectives and strategies.
7 Programmes with forecasts and budgets.

*This often causes confusion.

Try Exercise 2.2

Why do it?

As business becomes increasingly complex and competition increases, a marketing plan is essential.

The benefits are:

1   Better coordination of activities.
2   It identifies expected developments.
3   It increases organizational preparedness to change.
4   It minimizes non-rational responses to the unexpected.
5   It reduces conflicts about where the company should be going.
6   It improves communications.
7   Management is forced to think ahead systematically.
8   Available resources can be better matched to opportunities.
9   The plan provides a framework for the continuing review of operations.
10   A systematic approach to strategy formulation leads to a higher return on investment.

Try Exercise 2.3

Will it help us to survive?

All companies need to have a longer-term (strategic) marketing view as well as a short-term (tactical) marketing operation. Often the most potent short-term tactic is the use of the salesforce. These can combine thus:

	Market planning	
	Ineffective	Effective
Good	Die quickly	Thrive
Poor	Die slowly	Survive

Sales performance

From this it can be seen that being good at implementing the wrong strategy can lead to a very quick death!

Try Exercise 2.4

Questions raised for the company
---

1 Can we 'buy' an 'off the peg' planning system?

Since all companies are different, the process has to be 'tailored' to fit individual requirements.

2 Are we talking about tactics or strategy?

A strategic marketing plan takes a long-term look (say 3 years) and is therefore strategic. A tactical, or operational, marketing plan is a detailed scheduling and costing out of the *first* year of the strategic marketing plan.

3 How is the marketing plan used?

The plan determines where the company is now, where it wants to go and how to get there. It therefore should be the backdrop against which all organizational decisions are made.

4 Does the plan have to be written?

The planning sequence is really a thinking process. However, key pieces of information are worth writing down because they reduce confusion and aid communication. The degree of formality depends on the size of the company and the complexity of its business.

5 How detailed?

Enough to be useful.

Introduction

The first exercise in this chapter enables you to make an objective analysis of your company's marketing planning process. If you choose, you can then take matters further by working out in what ways the planning process might be improved.

The second exercise helps to clarify an often misunderstood issue, that of the company's mission statement.

The third exercise explores the extent to which your company is receiving the benefits that are usually attributed to a marketing planning process.

The final exercise will enable you to plot your company's position on the 'survival matrix'. There are several benefits to be derived from knowing this:

1 It infers the relation between your company's focus on long-term versus short-term issues.
2 It can be a powerful means of communicating to your colleagues that all might not be well in the company.
3 It provides an unambiguous message about what the company needs to address for future survival.

Exercise 2.1 The marketing planning process questionnaire

This questionnaire enables you to make an objective assessment about the marketing planning process in your company. It is designed to enable you to take a 'helicopter view' of the way your company does its planning and then to home in on the areas where improvements can be made. This approach will also enable you to identify information gaps that might be unknown to you at present.

Although care has been taken to use generally accepted terminology in the wording of this questionnaire, there will always be the company that uses different words. For example, when we talk about return on investment (ROI), other companies might well use other expressions or measures, such as return on capital employed, etc.

With this caveat in mind, please turn to the questionnaire and respond to it by putting a tick against each question in one of the four columns provided.

SCORING AND INTERPRETATION FOR EXERCISE 2.1

1   Add up how many ticks were listed under 'not applicable'. It is our experience that if there are more than eight ticks, then some aspects of planning that are covered by most companies are being avoided. Reappraise those items you initially ticked as 'not applicable'. Try getting a second opinion by checking your findings with colleagues.

2   Look at those items you ticked as 'don't know'. Find out if those activities are covered in your company's planning process.

3   Having ascertained what is and what isn't done in your company, list:

(a) The *good* things in your company's planning process.
(b) The *bad* things about it.

4   Make a note, in the space below, or on a separate sheet of paper, of ways in which you think the planning process in your company could be improved.

	Yes	No	Don't know	Not applic.

Section 1   Corporate issues

1   Is there a corporate statement about:

   (i) The nature of the company's current business mission?

   (ii) Its vision of the future?

2   Is there a target figure for ROI?

3   Is there a corporate plan to channel the company resources to this end?

4   Are there defined business boundaries in terms of:

   (i) Products or services (that will be offered)?

   (ii) Customers or markets (to deal with)?

   (iii) Production facilities?

   (iv) Distribution facilities?

   (v) Size and character of the workforce?

   (vi) Sources and levels of funding?

5   Are there objectives for promoting the corporate image with:

   (i) The stock market?

   (ii) Customers?

   (iii) The local community?

   (iv) The employees?

   (v) Environmentalist/conservationist lobby?

   (vi) Government departments?

   (vii) Trade associations, etc.?

Section 2   Marketing issues

6   Is there a marketing plan?

7   Is it compatible with the corporate plan?

8   Does it cover the same period?

9   Is the marketing plan regularly reviewed?

10   Is the plan based on an assessment of market potential or past performance?

11   Will the plan close the 'gap' if carried out?

12   Is there a marketing plan by product/service?

13   Do relevant managers have a copy of the marketing plan?

14   Are the following factors monitored in a regular and conscious way, in terms of how they affect the company's business prospects?

	Yes	No	Don't know	Not applic.

(a) Business environment

(i)   Economic factors?

(ii) Political/legal factors?

(iii) Fiscal factors

(iv) Technological developments?

(v)   Social/cultural factors?

(vi) Intra-company issues?

(b) The market

(i)   Trends in market size/growth in volume?
in value?

(ii) Developments/trends in product use?
product demand?
product presentation?
accessories?
substitutes?

(iii) Developments/trends in prices?
terms and conditions?
trade practices?

(iv) Developments/trends in physical distribution?
channels of distribution?
purchasing patterns?
stockholding?
turnover?

(v)   Developments/trends in communications?
use of salesforce?
advertising?
promotions?
exhibitions?

(c) Competition

(i)   Developments/trends of competitors?
their marketing strategies?
their strengths?
their weaknesses?
new entrants?
mergers/acquisitions?
their reputation?

(d) The industry

(i)   Activities of trade association(s)?

(ii)   Inter-firm comparisons

(iii) Industry profitability?

(iv)   Investment levels of competitors?

(v)   Changes in cost structure?

(vi)   Investment prospects?

(vii) Technological developments?

(viii) Sources of raw materials?

(ix)   Energy utilization?

	Yes	No	Don't know	Not applic.

Section 3   SWOT analysis

1   Is there someone (individual or group) responsible for converting the analysis of factors in Section 2 into a summary which highlights:

  (i) The company's principal strengths?

  (ii) The company's principal weaknesses (in terms of relating to external opportunities/threats)?

2   Does this person(s) have access to the necessary information?

3   Is this person (s) sufficiently senior for his analysis to make an impact?

4   Is the organizational climate such that a full and accurate analysis is seen as a striving for improvement rather than an attack on specific departments or vested interests?

Section 4   Assumptions

1   Is there a set of assumptions around which the marketing plan is formulated?

2   Are these assumptions made explicit to senior company personnel?

3   Do they cover:

  (i)   The business environment?

  (ii) The market?

  (iii) The competitors?

  (iv) The industry?

4   Are the assumptions valid in the light of current and predicted trading situations?

Section 5   Marketing objectives/strategies

1   Are the marketing objectives clearly stated and consistent with the corporate objectives?

2   Are there clear strategies for achieving the stated marketing objectives?

3   Are sufficient resources made available?

4   Are all responsibilities and authority clearly made known?

5   Are there agreed objectives about:

  (i)   The product range?

  (ii)   The value of sales?

  (iii) The volume of sales?

  (iv)   Profits?

  (v)   Market share?

  (vi)   Market penetration?

  (vii) Number of customers?

	Yes	No	Don't know	Not applic.
(viii) Introducing new products/services?	✓			
(ix) Divesting of old products/services?	✓			
(x) Organization changes to:				
(a) Develop company strengths?			✓	
(b) Reduce company weaknesses?			✓	

Section 6 Monitoring evaluation

	Yes	No	Don't know	Not applic.
1 Is the planning system well conceived and effective?	✓			
2 Do control mechanisms exist to ensure planned objectives are met?	✓			
3 Do internal communications function effectively?	✓			
4 Are there any problems between marketing and other corporate functions?		✓		
5 Are people clear about their role in the planning process?			✓	
6 Is there a procedure for dealing with non-achievement of objectives?	✓			
7 Is there evidence that this reduces the chance of subsequent failure?			✓	
8 Are there still unexploited opportunities?			✓	
9 Are there still organizational weaknesses?			✓	
10 Are the assumptions upon which the plan was based valid?			✓	
11 Are there contingency plans in the event of objectives not being met/conditions changing?			✓	

PERSONAL NOTES

Exercise 2.2 The mission statement

The following should appear in a mission statement:

1 *Role or contribution*
   - Profit (specify), or
   - Service, or
   - Opportunity-seeker.
2 *Business definition*
   This should be defined in terms of the *benefits* you provide or the *needs* you satisfy, rather than in terms of what you do or what you make.
3 *Distinctive competence*
   What essential skills/capabilities/resources underpin whatever success has been achieved to date? (*Note*: These factors should not apply equally to a competitor, otherwise there is no distinctive quality about them.)
4 *Indications for the future*
   - What the company *will* do.
   - What the company *might* do.
   - What the company will *never* do.

QUESTIONS

1 To what extent does your company's mission statement meet the criteria listed above?
2 If you do not have a mission statement, try writing one, following the guidelines provided here. Try it out on your colleagues and see if they agree with you or if they can find ways to improve on what you have written.

SCORING AND INTERPRETATION FOR EXERCISE 2.2

Use the following to gauge whether you feel you and your colleagues have developed a mission statement that is of real value:

- What values are true priorities for the next few years?

- What would make me professionally commit my mind and heart to this vision over the next 5 to 10 years?
- What is unique about us?
- What does the world really need that our company can and should provide?
- What do I want our company to accomplish so that I will be committed, aligned, and proud of my association with the institution?

Exercise 2.3   The benefits of marketing planning

What follows is a list of the benefits of marketing planning. With your company in mind, score each benefit by means of the scale given below.

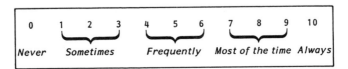

1 Our approach to marketing planning ensures that we get a high level of coordination of our various marketing activities.   . . . .

2 Our marketing planning process enables us to identify unexpected developments in advance.   . . . .

3 Because of the way we approach marketing planning, there is an increased readiness for the organization to change, in response to the issues 'flagged up'.   . . . .

4 When we are faced with the unexpected, our marketing planning process minimizes the risk of non-rational responses.   . . . .

5 Having a marketing plan reduces the conflicts between managers regarding 'where the company should be going'.   . . . .

6 Our marketing plan improves communications about market-related issues.   . . . .

7 Because of our marketing planning process, management is forced to think ahead systematically.   . . . .

8 Having a marketing plan enables us to match our resources to opportunities in an effective way.   . . . .

9 Our marketing plan provides us with a useful framework for a continuing review of progress.   . . . .

10 Our marketing planning has led us to develop more profitable marketing strategies.   . . . .

TOTAL   _____

SCORING AND INTERPRETATION FOR EXERCISE 2.3

The maximum score for the exercise is 100. If you scored:

81–100: Marketing planning is really paying off in your company.

61–80: You are not receiving the benefits you should be receiving. What's getting in the way? (Exercise 2.1 might give some clues.)

41–60: You appear to be moving along the right lines, but there is still a long way to go.

0–40: Either your marketing planning process is inadequate, or your company is not really trying to make marketing planning work.

Exercise 2.4   Survival matrix

Before you tackle this exercise, it is important to remember that profitability and high market growth are nearly always correlated. In other words, the higher the market growth, the higher the profitability.

This phenomenon can sometimes obscure the fact that a company that appears to be doing well can still be losing ground in comparison with its competitors. While apparently thriving, it is in fact dying slowly. The crunch comes when the erstwhile buoyant market growth slows down, and the other companies demonstrate quite clearly their superior performance.

INSTRUCTIONS

Before coming to the matrix, please respond to the following statements by scoring them as follows:

0	1 2 3	4 5 6	7 8 9	10
Never	*Sometimes*	*Frequently*	*Most of the time*	*Always*

1   When it comes to recruiting salespeople, we seem able to pick the best candidates in the job market.   ....

2   The training we provide for salespeople is second to none.   ....

3   Our salespeople consistently meet or exceed their sales targets.   ....

4   Compared with our competitors, our salespeople have a better image.   ....

5   We actually have the most appropriate number of salespeople employed.   ....

6   Our sales staff are clear about the role they are expected to play.   ....

7   Our sales managers are very good motivators.   ....

8   Territory planning is a strong point of our salesforce.   ....

9   The salesforce has a good conversion rate in terms of number of visits per order.   ....

10   Our sales force is reasonably stable, i.e. there is not a labour turnover problem.   ....

TOTAL   _____

SCORING AND INTERPRETATION FOR EXERCISE 2.4

Enter the salesforce effectiveness score on the vertical axis on the matrix (Figure 2.1) and then draw a horizontal dotted line across the matrix. Take the marketing benefits score from Exercise 2.3 and enter this on the horizontal axis of the matrix. Draw a vertical dotted line up from this point.

Where the two dotted lines meet is where you position your company on the survival matrix.

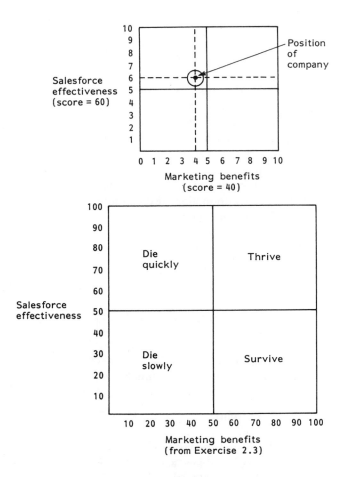

Figure 2.1 *Survival matrix*

QUESTIONS

1 What are the implications for your company?
2 What actions might be required if improvements are needed?

3 Removing the barriers to marketing planning

Ignorance

Most companies plan, using a combination of forecasting and budgeting systems. These tend to project current business into the future, which can work if the future is going to be the same as the present or the past. As a result of using such systems, the following problems often occur:

1 Lost opportunities for profit.
2 Meaningless numbers in long-term plans.
3 Unrealistic objectives.
4 Lack of actionable market information.
5 Interfunctional strife.
6 Management frustration.
7 Proliferation of products and markets.
8 Wasted promotional expenditure.
9 Confusion over pricing.
10 Growing vulnerability to changes in the business environment.
11 Loss of control over the business.

Try Exercise 3.1

Common implementation problems

---

1 Weak support from the chief executive and top management.
2 Lack of a plan for planning.
3 Lack of line management support due to:

- Hostility.
- Lack of skills.
- Lack of resources.
- Lack of information.
- Inadequate organization structure.

4 Confusion over planning terms.
5 Numbers in lieu of written objectives and strategies.
6 Too much detail, too far ahead.
7 Once-a-year ritual.

8 Separation of operational marketing planning from strategic marketing planning.
9 Failure to integrate marketing planning into the total corporate planning system.
10 Delegation of planning to a planner.

Try Exercise 3.2

| *Questions raised for the company* |

1 If we introduce marketing planning, will we automatically become more successful?

No. Many other factors come into play.
2 What are these factors?

Here are three common factors:

(*a*) Companies who by chance are in high growth markets often don't plan. They are just dragged along by the general momentum.
(*b*) If the company's culture and management style are not really supportive of marketing planning (i.e. there is no real belief in it), no improvements will occur.
(*c*) If the business is highly competitive, no improvement will necessarily be seen. *But* the company might fare much worse without a marketing plan.
3 Is all the time and effort put into marketing planning going to be worthwhile?

Only you can say. Weigh up the costs of planning against the costs of not planning.

Introduction

The first exercise in this section focuses on the types of problem that your company might be experiencing because of inefficiencies in the marketing planning system. In this sense it is providing an additional diagnosis about whether or not you need to improve your system. At the same time it helps to uncover some of the areas on which any new planning process needs to make an impact.

The second exercise attempts to be quite specific in pinpointing which aspects of the company need to be addressed in order to bring about the biggest improvements in marketing planning.

Exercise 3.1 Symptoms of a lack of marketing planning

Put an 'X' at the point you feel is appropriate as being descriptive of your company against each of the statements below:

	Mainly true	Mainly untrue
1 We seem to be missing opportunities for making profit.		
2 Our long-term planning seems to be nothing more than lots of meaningless numbers.		
3 Looked at rationally, our marketing objectives are unreasonable.		
4 We lack actionable marketing information.		
5 Managers are frustrated by the interfunctional strife and rivalry which seem to exist.		
6 There seems to be a steady proliferation of products and/or markets.		
7 Much of our promotional expenditure is wasted.		
8 There is confusion over pricing.		
9 We are becoming increasingly vulnerable to changes in our business environment.		
10 There is a feeling that we are not running the business, but instead, it and outside forces are running us.		

If you find it difficult to put an 'X' against any statement, you should confer with some colleagues rather than making guesses.

Join the 'X' for statement 1 to the 'X' of statement 2 with a straight line. Then join 2 to 3, 3 to 4, etc. in a similar way down to 10.

INTERPRETATION OF EXERCISE 3.1

You have just drawn a 'profile' of 'marketing planning' in your company.

- If your 'profile line' tends to be positioned to the right-hand side of the spectrum, then it appears that you are not experiencing many of the problems which stem from a lack of marketing planning. In other words, you appear to be doing things fairly well.
- If, on the other hand, your profile line tends towards the left-hand side, you are much less fortunate, and should consider reviewing your current marketing planning process, paying particular attention to the problems you wish to overcome.

Exercise 3.2 Marketing planning questionnaire — organizational issues

You are asked to answer a series of statements about your organization's approach to marketing planning. Since this quest is for useful and genuine data, please try to be as accurate and objective as you can as you complete this document.

You score the questionnaire by entering a number, 1–5, *only in the position indicated by the dotted line next to each statement.* Choose your scores, using these criteria:

A   If you strongly disagree with statement.
B   If you tend to disagree with statement.
C   If you don't know if you agree or disagree.
D   If you tend to agree with statement.
E   If you strongly agree with statement.

THE RATIONALE BEHIND THE QUESTIONNAIRE

There are many ways of looking at organizations and establishing 'models' of how they operate. One very common model is the organization chart, which attempts to show how responsibility is distributed throughout the company and to clarify the chains of command.

Other models are derived from the inputs and outputs of the company. For example, a financial model is built up by analysing all the necessary financial inputs required to conduct the business and monitoring the efficiency by which these are converted into sales revenue.

The questionnaire in Exercise 3.2 is based on a particularly useful model, one which helps us to understand the relation between different facets of the organization. By understanding the nature of these relations, we are better placed to introduce organizational change – in this case, an improved marketing planning system.

There are three main assumptions behind this model:

1   *That the organization today is to some extent, often very strongly, conditioned by its historical background.* For example, if historically there has never been a pressing need for a comprehensive

You are asked to answer a series of statements about your organization's approach to marketing planning. Since this quest is for useful and genuine data, please try to be as accurate and objective as you can as you complete this document.

You score the questionnaire by entering a number, 1–5, *only in the position indicated by the dotted line next to each statement.* Choose your scores, using these criteria:

A	B	C	D	E
If you strongly disagree with statement	If you tend to disagree with statement	If you don't know if you agree or disagree	If you tend to agree with statement	If you strongly agree with statement

	A	B	C	D	E
1 The chief executive directors show an active interest in marketing planning.					--
2 The chief executive directors demonstrate their understanding of marketing planning.	--				
3 The chief executive directors use the marketing plan as the basis for making key marketing decisions.				--	
4 The chief executive directors allocate adequate resources to ensure the marketing plan is completed satisfactorily.			--		
5 The need for a marketing plan is clearly explained to all managers.	--				
6 There is adequate information/data upon which to base a marketing plan.			--		
7 Our marketing plan has a good balance between short-term and long-term objectives.				--	
8 People are clear about their role in the marketing planning process.					--
9 Line managers are trained to understand how the marketing planning process operates.	--				
10 Line operational managers believe the marketing plan is a useful document.				--	
11 Enough time is allowed for the planning process.			--		
12 It is made easy for line managers to understand the plan.	--				
13 Marketing planning is never starved for lack of resources.			--		
14 It is reasonable for a company like ours to have a well-thought-out marketing plan.				--	

	A	B	C	D	E
15 Reasons for past successes or failures are analysed.			--		
16 In our organization we don't leave planning just to the planners; other managers have a valuable contribution to make.					--
17 Our organizational style encourages a sound marketing planning process.				--	
18 There is a clear understanding of the marketing terminology we use in our organization.	--				
19 Market opportunities are highlighted by the planning process.			--		
20 Functional specialists contribute to the marketing planning process.					--
21 We limit our activities so that we are not faced with trying to do too many things at one time.		--			
22 Taking part in marketing planning in our organization holds a high prospect of being rewarded, either financially or in career terms.				--	
23 Only essential data appear in our plans.		--			
24 Marketing does not operate in an 'ivory tower'.				--	
25 From the wealth of information available to use, we are good at picking out the key issues.	--				
26 There is a balance between narrative explanation and numerical data in our plans.				--	
27 Our field salesforce operates in a way which is supportive to our marketing plan.					--
28 Our plan demonstrates a high level of awareness of the 'macro' issues facing us.	--				
29 Inputs to the planning process are on the whole as accurate as we can make them.		--			
30 Marketing planning is always tackled in a meaningful and serious way.				--	
31 Our plan doesn't duck the major problems and opportunities faced by the organization.				--	
32 There is a high awareness of 'micro' issues in our plan.	--				
33 Our plans recognize that in the short term we have to match our current capabilities to the market opportunities.		--			
34 Inputs to the marketing planning process are an integral part of the job of all line managers.					--

	A	B	C	D	E
35 Marketing planning is a priority issue in our organization.				--	
36 Our planning inputs are not 'massaged' to satisfy senior executives.		--			
37 People understand and are reasonably happy that our marketing planning process is logical and appropriate.	--				
38 We use the same time-scale for our marketing plans as we do for finance, distribution, production and personnel.			--		
39 We view our operational plan as the first year of our long-term plan, not as a separate entity.			--		
40 Senior executives do not see themselves as operating beyond the confines of the marketing plan.				--	
41 The advocates of 'correct' marketing planning are senior enough in the company to make sure it happens.				--	
42 People are always given clear instructions about the nature of their expected contribution to the marketing plan.					--
43 We try to make data collection and retrieval as simple as possible.			--		
44 Our marketing plans do not go into great detail, but usually give enough information to make any necessary point.			--		
45 The role of specialists is made quite clear in our planning process.					--
46 We are always prepared to learn any new techniques that will make our marketing planning process more effective.	--				
47 The role of marketing planning is clearly understood in the organization.					--
48 Marketing research studies (by internal staff or agencies) are often used as inputs to our marketing planning process.		--			
49 Our marketing planning is regularly evaluated in an attempt to improve the process.			--		
50 The chief executive directors receive information which enables them to assess whether or not the marketing plan is coming to fruition as expected.					--
TOTAL SCORES					

marketing planning system because of favourable trading conditions, then this will be reflected in the current planning system and the attitudes of the company's staff.

2 *That the organization today is to some extent, sometimes strongly, conditioned and directed by its future goals.* For example, the company that senses its marketing planning processes need to improve will take steps to introduce changes. That these changes will make an impact on organizational life is self-evident. Furthermore, much of the resistance to be overcome will stem from the 'historical' forces mentioned above.

3 *What actually happens in an organization is determined by the skills, knowledge, experience and beliefs of the organization's personnel.* Thus at the heart of any organization is the collective expertise or 'education' at its disposal. This will ultimately determine the success it has in any work it undertakes, whether it is making goods or providing services.

Clearly then, the level of 'education' will also be a determining factor in the quality and scope of the company's marketing planning process. These assumptions provide the 'skeleton' of our organizational model (Figure 3.1).

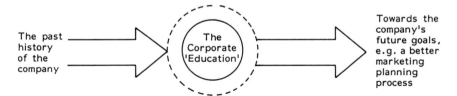

Figure 3.1 *Education and marketing planning*

There are still important elements missing from this model. Irrespective of the company's corporate sum of available skills and knowledge, nothing can be produced without physical *resources* being made available. The key resources required for marketing planning will be accurate data, means of storing and retrieving the data, adequate staff and time to analyse the data.

But having the right resources isn't the whole solution; the company must also develop the best systems or *routines* to optimize the use of these resources. In marketing planning terms, concern is likely to focus on routines associated with collecting data, evaluating past performance, spotting marketing opportunities, sifting essential information from non-essential information, etc.

Routines however do not necessarily look after themselves. As soon as any system is set up, *roles and relationships* need to be defined. Who is going to do what to ensure that things happen?

Again, in marketing planning terms this will call into question the role of various members of staff from the chief executive downwards. How clear are people about their role in the planning process? Should planning just be left to the planning department. What is the role of functional specialists? Who actually collects marketing data? Whom do they present it to? Many questions have to be answered if the subsequent routines are going to function smoothly.

Even this isn't the end of the story, because once roles are defined, there is still the problem of setting up the right *organizational structure and climate*, one that will enable people to fulfil their roles in a productive way.

From a marketing-planning viewpoint, structure and climate issues surface in several ways. For example, the level of commitment to the planning process, the degree to which functional specialists are integrated into the planning process, the degree to which long- and short-term issues are accommodated, the extent to which the company is prepared to tackle the real and important issues it faces, the openness of communications, etc.

It is now possible to see how the completed model looks (Figure 3.2).

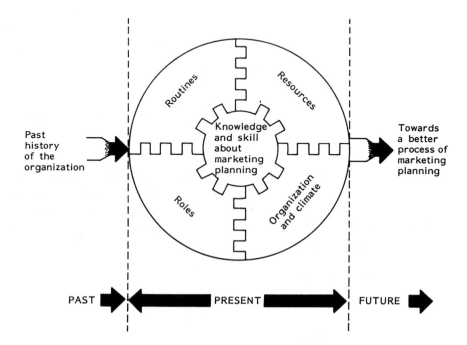

Figure 3.2   *Marketing planning model*

From the foregoing explanation, it is possible to see how the different facets of the organization

(a) the 'corporate education', about marketing planning;
(b) the resources allocated to planning;
(c) the routines or systems that are used;
(d) the roles and relationships of those engaged in marketing planning;
(e) the organizational structure and climate, and the extent to which
  it supports marketing planning;

all interrelate. Thus to introduce an improved marketing planning system might call for changes in all these areas. Some personnel might need training, more or different resources might be required, routines or systems might need improving, roles and relationships perhaps need to be reappraised, and the structure and climate of the organization re-examined.

Conversely, only one or two of these areas might need tackling.

The questionnaire is designed to provide a 'snapshot' of the company and to help you identify which areas might be the starting point for introducing improvements.

INTERPRETATION OF EXERCISE 3.2

Add up the scores for columns **A, B, C, D** and **E** and write them in the boxes provided. Each of the letters represents a potential barrier to marketing planning, namely:

A = Cognitive barrier, i.e. knowledge and skills.
B = Resource barrier, i.e. lack of time, people, data.
C = Systems/routine barrier, i.e. lack of procedures.
D = Organizational climate barrier, i.e. belief and interest in marketing planning.
E = Behaviour barrier, i.e. the roles people play.

The maximum score for each of these areas is 50 points. The higher the score, the less that potential barrier to marketing is likely to be making an impact. In other words, the areas with low scores (below 30) will probably be the areas worth investigating initially in the search for improvement.

PERSONAL NOTES

List what actions need to be taken?

4 The customer and the market audit

| Customers or consumers? |

Customers are people who buy from you. *Consumers* are the users of your products or services, e.g. husband (customer) buys perfume for wife (consumer). Sometimes the customer is also the consumer. Marketers need to know about the characteristics of both if they are to develop the best 'package' to meet their needs.

| Market share |

Market share is a key concept in marketing. It is the proportion of *actual* sales (either volume or value) within a defined market. How the company defines its market is extremely critical.

Try Exercise 4.1

Research shows that there is a direct correlation between market share and profitability.

| Critical success factors |

Within any given market segment there are critical success factors (CSFs) for winning the business, e.g. reliable delivery, acceptable design, low running costs, and so on. It will be essential for the company to establish what these are *and* how well it compares with its closest competitors, when measured against these factors.

Try Exercise 4.2

| Market segmentation |

A market segment is a group of customers with similar characteristics who share similar needs. A company generally cannot deal successfully with a large number of segments – it would lead to fragmentation of effort. Therefore it should deal with a limited number of segments which meet these criteria:

- Each segment is sufficiently large to give the company a return for its effort.
- Members of each segment have a high degree of similarity.
- The criteria for describing the segment must relate to the buying situation.
- The segment must be reachable.

Segmentation can be based on a combination of:

1 Analysis of customer behaviour:

   (a) What do they buy and why?

   - value/volume,
   - price,
   - frequency,
   - where they buy/outlet,
   - products/services etc.

Try Exercise 4.3

   (b) Why do they buy?

   - benefits,
   - lifestyle,
   - fashion/novelty,
   - personality types,
   - peer-group pressure,
   - preferences, etc.

Try Exercise 4.4

2 Analysis of customer characteristics (what they are)

   - customer size,
   - socioeconomic groups,
   - demographic considerations,
   - industrial classification,
   - cultural/geographic factors.

Try Exercise 4.5

Questions raised for the company
---

1   Why is market segmentation so important?

Few companies can be 'all things to all men'. Segmentation allows the firm to target its effort on the most promising opportunities.

2   How can we be expected to know our market share?

The more accurately you can define your market segments, the more accurately you will find you can measure your market share. Correct market definition is also critical for:

- Growth measurement.
- Specifying target customers.
- Recognizing relevant competitors.
- Setting marketing objectives and strategies.

3   How can we keep tabs on all our competitors?

You don't have to – just concentrate on your closest competitors and try to ensure that you maintain some differential advantage over them.

Introduction

Exercise 4.1 looks at the most crucial and complex issue in marketing, i.e. how a market is defined. Until this is clearly understood, issues such as market share, the identification of target customers and their needs, and even the recognition of competitors, will continuously cause difficulty.

Exercise 4.2 examines critical success factors.

Exercise 4.3 provides a technique for auditing industrial goods and services.

Exercise 4.4 introduces another technique, benefit analysis, and this is extended and put into practice in Exercise 4.5, which provides a case study for analysis.

There is also some supplementary material in this section which could help you with your own customer and market audits. It comprises:

1   *Customer classification systems*
    (*a*)   Social Grading on National Research Surveys.
    (*b*)   Hall-Jones Classification.
    (*c*)   Family Life Cycle.
    (*d*)   Registrar-General's 'Social Class'.
2   *Standard Industrial Classification*

Exercise 4.1 Market definition

Often there is confusion regarding what constitutes a market. Unless such confusion is dispelled from the outset, the whole marketing edifice will be built on sand. However, as so often is the case, what on the surface appears to be a relatively simple task can prove to be extremely testing. Take this example, which vastly simplifies the problem.

XYZ Ltd has five major products, A, B, C, D and E, which are sold to five different markets, as represented in the Figure 4.1. Virtually all sales are achieved in the shaded areas.

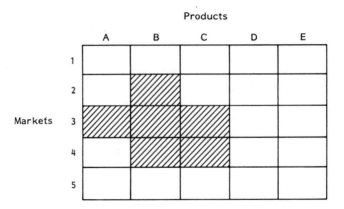

Figure 4.1 *Example of market definition*

Is this company's market:

(*a*) The shaded areas?
(*b*) The intersection of products A, B and C and markets 2, 3 and 4?
(*c*) Products A, B and C for all markets?
(*d*) Markets 2, 3 and 4 for all products?
(*e*) The entire matrix?

INTERPRETATION AND SCORING FOR EXERCISE 4.1

1 It would be possible to define our market as the shaded areas ((*a*) in the exercise), i.e. the product/market area currently served.

The problem with this is that it might tend to close our eyes to other potential opportunities for profitable growth and expansion, especially if there is a danger that our current markets may become mature.

2   It is also possible to define our market as the intersection of products A, B and C and markets 2, 3 and 4 ((*b*) in the exercise). The problem with this is that while we now have a broader vision, there may be developments in product areas D and E and markets 1 and 5 that we should be aware of.

3   To a large extent, this problem would be overcome by defining our market as products A, B and C for *all* markets ((*c*) in the exercise). The problem here is that markets 1 and 5 may not require products A, B and C, so perhaps we need to consider product development (products D and E).

4   It is certainly possible to consider our market as all products for markets 2, 3 and 4 ((*d*) in the exercise). The potential problem here is that we still do not have any interest in markets 1 and 3.

5   Finally, it is clearly possible to call the entire matrix our market ((*e*) in the exercise), with markets 1 to 5 on the vertical axis and each of products A to E on the horizontal axis. The problem with this is that we would almost certainly have too many markets, or segments, and this could lead to a costly dissipation of effort.

The answer to the conundrum therefore is that it is purely a matter of management judgement. Any combinations of (*a*)-(*e*) above could be used as long as there is a sensible rationale to justify the choice. In addition, please remember the following useful definition of market segmentation: 'An identifiable group of customers with requirements in common that are, or may become, significant in terms of developing a separate strategy'.

Often the way a market was selected in the first instance can provide clues regarding how it can be defined. Generally, either consciously or intuitively, a screening process is used to eliminate unsuitable markets and to arrive at those with potential. This screening process often works something like that shown in Figure 4.2.

Consider one of your current markets and explain:

1   How it came to be chosen.
2   How you would define it, so that it is clearly distinct from any other market.

Please remember that the crude method outlined above, while working at a very general level, rarely leads to the development of differential advantage, and it is suggested that the other exercises in this chapter

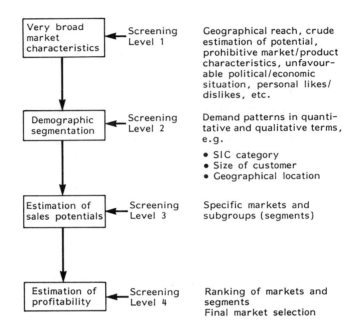

Figure 4.2   *Market screening*

should be completed in order to get a better understanding of the central significance of market segmentation in marketing success.

Exercise 4.2 Critical success factors (CSFs)

Critical success factors can vary from one type of business to another, or indeed from one market segment to another. Therefore it is impossible to be prescriptive about your CSFs, and you will have to draw on the expertise you have about your business and establish which ones are correct for you.

Remember a CSF is something which helps you to clinch the business. Thus, by definition, if it were absent, your success rate would plummet.

Normally there would only be a few CSFs, probably not more than five, although there might be many other factors which contribute to success.

Table 4.1 is an example of the way a firm of quantity surveyors analysed their business.

Table 4.1

CSF		*Weighting*	*Score out of 10 (10 = very high standard)*	*Adjusted score**
1	Early identification of building contracts	0.5	6	30
2	Track record of performance	0.3	6	18
3	Quality of sales staff	0.2	8	16
		1.0		64%

* Adjusted score = score out of 10 × weighting factor

Weighting factors are distributed to each CSF according to their relative importance. In Table 4.1 CSF1 is the most important, but the company only scores 6, just over average. In contrast, on CSF3, the company scores high, but this factor is the least critical of those listed and so the net result is diminished.

The company now repeats this process (Table 4.2), this time focusing on its nearest competitors.

On the evidence in Table 4.2 our company can see that Competitor A, even with a lower quality salesforce and a slightly poorer track record, has a competitive advantage because of its ability to identify potential

Table 4.2

CSF	Weighting	Comp. A score		Comp. B score		Comp. C score	
		Raw	Adjusted	Raw	Adjusted	Raw	Adjusted
1	0.5	9	45	5	25	7	35
2	0.3	5	15	5	15	7	21
3	0.2	6	12	5	10	5	10
			72%		50%		66%

contracts earlier. Similarly, Competitor C is a force to be reckoned with. In contrast, Competitor B has a lot of ground to make up in all areas.

This technique can be applied to all companies and provides three useful outcomes:

1 It forces people to think about their critical success factors.
2 It provides an overview of relative competitiveness when measured against their main competitors.
3 It highlights the areas where the most effective improvements might be made.

Now try it on your company. See Tables 4.3 and 4.4.

Table 4.3

CSF	Weighting	Score out of 10 (10 = very high standard)	Adjusted score
CSF1			
CSF2			
CSF3			
CSF4			
CSF5			

Table 4.4

CSF	Weighting	Comp. A score		Comp. B score		Comp. C score	
		Raw	Adjusted	Raw	Adjusted	Raw	Adjusted
CSF1							
CSF2							
CSF3							
CSF4							
CSF5							

Exercise 4.3   Market audit — industrial goods and services

Using your own company as the study vehicle, please complete the market audit form (Table 4.5) by following these instructions:

Step 1	In column 1 list all those industries that are consumers of your goods or services. Please note that there is no need to structure this list, just write them down as they occur to you. Refer to the Standard Industrial Classification if it helps you to categorize the industries (see p. 77).
Step 2	In column 2 write the actual turnover figure.
Step 3	In column 3 write down the percentage value of turnover that results from each of the industries.
Step 4	In column 4 indicate whether or not this, when considered from the point of view of profitability, is high or low, by scoring 10 for high, 5 for good, and 1 for low. (Here 'profitability' means whatever your company considers it to mean.)
Step 5	Using column 5, consider what capacity and skills you have at your disposal to continue supplying each industry. A score of 10 would show you have considerable capacity, with minimal interference to other products or services: 1 would indicate severe limitations.
Step 6	Using a similar scoring procedure, complete column 6. Ask yourself how confident is your company that it can supply each industry with the right quality and design of goods/services, delivered on time. Are you more confident about some than others?
Step 7	Now consider the market potential (demand) for your output in each of the listed industries. Using column 7, score 10 for high potential and 1 for low.
Step 8	Add the scores you have allocated in columns 4, 5, 6, 7, and enter them in column 8.
Step 9	Using the information you have put together, identify your key market segments. They ought to be those industries which collected the highest aggregate scores, but for your type of business you might identify other factors that would influence your choice of market. Make a note of these in

column 9. In addition, use column 9 to record any particular opportunities or threats presented in each market.

Step 10   Balancing the notes you made in column 9 against the arithmetic calculations (column 8), study the information you have assembled, and select what you regard as the best industrial market. Enter 1 against this in column 10. Continue ranking each industry, using 2 for the next best, 3 for the third, etc., until column 10 is filled.

Information from this market audit could be used at a later state, when marketing objectives and strategies are examined (Exercises 6.6 and 6.7).

Table 4.5   **Market audit industrial goods and services**

1	2	3	4	5	6	7	8	9	10
Industry	Actual T/O	% T/O	Profitability L1 10H	Capacity L1 10H	Confidence L1 10H	Potential L1 10H	Total (Cols 4, 5,6,7)	Additional factors, oppor- tunities/threats	Rank

Exercise 4.4 Benefit analysis

Customers buy products and services because they seek to acquire a range of benefits which go with them. In this sense, all products and services are problem-solvers. Thus customers buy aspirin to solve the problem of headaches, they buy drills because they need holes, they buy convenience foods because they solve the problem of there not being enough hours in the day.

It is essential for providers of products or services to be aware that their output is only saleable for as long as it provides the benefits the customer requires, and for as long as it is seen by the customer to be good value when compared with other possible methods of solving their problems. Once there is a better, cheaper, quicker, tidier, more enjoyable way of putting holes in walls, the drill manufacturer will go the way of the buggy-whip maker. Therefore it is vitally important to know just as much about the benefits they supply as it is to know about the products or services themselves.

STANDARD BENEFITS

These are provided by the product but are not in any way unique, e.g. 'the propellent in our aerosol does not damage the ozone layer'. Although in this respect your product might be like all others, not to make customers aware of this standard benefit could imply that you still use environmentally unfriendly materials. Clearly this would be to your disadvantage.

COMPANY BENEFITS

The business transaction links the customer to the company. In turn, this means that there ought to be some benefits to that customer for making that choice. Customers will prefer to deal with companies that provide better customer service, inspire confidence, have a reputation for fair trading policies, and so on. Company benefits are a means of differentiating your products or services from competing ones, if to all intents and purposes they are similar. For example, some banks are trying to establish specific identities to the benefits they supply. Hence there is 'the listening bank' and 'the bank that likes to say yes'. Perhaps eventually there will be 'the bank that is open when its customers want it to be'!

DIFFERENTIAL BENEFITS

These are the benefits that only your products or services provide. It is these that give the company its competitive advantage. It is these that must be identified, developed and exploited if the company is to win success. Here are some examples:

- 'We are the only company that provides a genuine 24-hour breakdown service. Therefore, any time you need us, we are there to get you moving again.'
- 'This is the only product on the market with this self-cleaning facility, so you can install it and have no maintenance worries.'

Not every benefit will have equal appeal to all customers, or groups of customers. However, by talking to them, or carrying out research, it ought to be possible to establish which are the important benefits in their eyes.

It is now possible to prepare a systematic benefit analysis along the lines shown in these examples. See Table 4.6.

Note
1   To get from a feature to an advantage, and then to a benefit, the phrase 'which means that' can be helpful, e.g. 'It's coated in new formula paint (feature) which means that the colour will never fade (advantage)'. If you *know* this is what the customer *needs*, then you have also arrived at a *benefit*.
2   To check if you have arrived at a benefit and not just an advantage, apply the 'so what?' test. Ask this question after the benefit. If the 'so what?' prompts you to go further, the chances are you have not yet reached the real benefit, e.g. 'Our products are hand-made (feature), which means they are better quality than machine-made ones (benefit?)' – 'so what?' – 'which means they last longer (the real benefit)'.

Now try producing a benefit analysis for one of your own products or services, as it impacts on a specific customer or customer group. Use Table 4.7.

Table 4.6

Customer (s)......................................

Service/product..................................

Customer appeal	Features	Advantages	Benefits	Proof
What issues are of particular concern to the customer, e.g. cost, reliability, safety, simplicity etc.?	What features of the product/ service best illustrate these issues? How do they work?	What advantages do these features provide, i.e. what do they do for the customer?	How can tangible benefits be expressed to give maximum customer appeal, i.e. what does the customer get that he/ she *needs*?	What evidence can be pro- vided to back up the benefit and show it can be attained?

Example – saucepans

Customer appeal	Features	Advantages	Benefits	Proof
Ease of use, ease of washing-up	Teflon-coated	This is a non-stick material	Trouble-free cooking, quicker washing-up	Results of tests

Example – office services bureau

Customer appeal	Features	Advantages	Benefits	Proof
Accuracy and speedy turn- round of work	We use the latest equipment and very skilled staff	We are extremely versatile	Minimum of errors, cost-saving	What customers say

Table 4.7

Customer(s) ------------------------------------

Service/product-----------------------------------

Customer appeal	Features	Advantages	Benefits	Proof

Exercise 4.5 The customer audit – Car Mart Ltd

As a prerequisite to establishing marketing objectives for your company, it will be important to analyse the customers of your products or services. For some businesses it is adequate to focus on the needs of groups of individual customers; for others it is more important to look at customers as being whole industries. In this exercise we will concentrate on the former type of customer base.

The information you assemble by completing this exercise can be used at a later stage of the marketing planning process.

TYPES OF CUSTOMER AUDIT

There are many different ways of auditing customers. Most of them work on the premise that customer needs will, to a large extent, be influenced by personal circumstances such as age, personality, occupation, lifestyle and financial situation. On pp. 59 – 63 you will find examples of four widely accepted classification systems based on socioeconomic or lifestyle criteria.

The following exercise will give you an opportunity to explore the practical implications of using one such approach.

CAR MART OBJECTIVE

Car Mart produces a record of a series of sales transactions from which you have to identify the key market segment(s) and useful customer audit material.

MATERIALS FOR CAR MART

1   *Twelve customer cards* (to be cut out from the back of the book), consisting of:

- A lift attendant.
- A bricklayer.
- A self-employed plumber.
- A bank manager (local branch).

- A computer programmer.
- A sales manager.
- A school teacher.
- A chairman of an industrial group.
- A senior partner in a firm of solicitors.
- A tool-maker.
- A factory machine operator.
- An elderly grannie.

2 *Six product cards – the showroom* (to be cut out from the back of the book) – consisting of:

- Economy car.
- Family saloon.
- Executive transport.
- Estate car.
- Second car.
- Sports car.

3 *Car Mart sales record sheet* (p. 55).

4 *Two dice* (these are not provided).

ASSUMPTIONS

This simulation does not attempt to portray real life in accurate detail, but merely to be the vehicle for learning, and thereby provide an opportunity for experimentation. To this end, the following assumptions are made:

1 Anyone tackling this exercise will have completed Exercise 4.4 or have a clear understanding about the difference between features and benefits.
2 The 'customers' in Car Mart have the financial resources to make their purchases.
3 The 'customer needs' expressed are a genuine attempt to reflect the likely views of that particular 'customer'.
4 The car 'chosen' is in an acceptable condition for the customer, i.e. it is new if the customer wants new, or second-hand if that is what the customer is looking for.

GENERATING THE DATA FOR CAR MART

There are two methods of developing the necessary data for this exercise:

1   Procedure for a group of four 'players'

(*a*) A group of four players is seated at a suitable table.

(*b*) The twelve customer cards are shuffled by Player 1 and then laid face up on the table in a vertical column by one of the players. The six product cards are also placed on the table in a separate group, face upwards, to represent the Car Mart showroom.

(*c*) Player 2, on the left of Player 1, shakes the two dice and uses the aggregate score to designate a customer card, e.g. if the dice showed 8 as a total score, Player 2 counts down the column of customer cards to the *eighth* card.

(*d*) Player 2 then imagines he is this customer and improvises a realistic buying need of that person by saying 'I'm looking for a car that (own words)', e.g. 'I'm looking for a car that will always start in the mornings'.

(*e*) Player 3 responds to this by selecting one of the product cards from the table (showroom), and explains a feature of this particular car by saying 'This one has (own words)', e.g. 'This car has been on the market for many years'.

(*f*) Player 4 then has to add a benefit statement to the feature raised by Player 3, by saying 'Which means that (own words)', e.g. 'Which means that it is now a very reliable vehicle'.

(*g*) One of the players (probably the neatest writer) then fills in the first transaction row of the 'sales record sheet' (p. 55), at this stage ignoring columns 2, 4 and 9, the narrow ones.

(*h*) This whole procedure is repeated, this time Player 3 shaking the dice and being the customer.

(*i*) This rotation of starter continues until twenty sales transactions have been completed, i.e. the sales record sheet is filled.

2   Procedure for individual study

If it is not possible to work in a group of four as described, an individual can work through the Car Mart exercise alone. He or she will of course have to play the role of each player described above. Nevertheless, this process will produce the completed sales record sheet, which is an essential prerequisite for this exercise. If it is possible, procedure 1 is recommended, because, with other people, the exercise becomes much more creative and stimulating.

Once the sales record sheet is completed, answer the questions in the next sections.

CAR MART SALES RECORD SHEET

1	2	3	4	5	6	7	8	9
Customer		Needs		Product	New or S/H	Feature	Benefit	

S/H = second-hand

THE CUSTOMER AUDIT (SOCIOECONOMIC GROUPS AND BUYING MOTIVES)

Imagine that the sales record sheet you have just completed was multiplied tenfold. In other words, it is a record of 200 sales transactions, which represents Car Mart's trading for the last year.

Working in the same group as that which generated the data for the sales record sheet, proceed as follows:

1   Decide into which socioeconomic category each customer falls. Enter your decisions in Column 2 of the sales record sheet.
2   Look at customer needs (Column 3) and decide which are *R*ational and which are more *P*sychological. Enter R or P in Column 4.
3   Similarly, look at benefits (Column 8) and enter R or P in Column 9, depending on whether or not the benefit is likely to appeal to the 'rational customer' or to his/her psychological needs.
4   Tick all those benefits where the R or P in Column 9 matches up with an R or P in Column 4.
5   Consider the ease/difficulty of completing 1 to 4 above, and reconcile any differences that occurred between Columns 4 and 9.
6   If time permits, you can discuss any interesting points which came out of the Car Mart sales record sheet.
7   When you have completed these tasks, proceed to the next section.

THE CUSTOMER AUDIT (SEGMENTATION)

Staying in the same group as before, use the information you have collected on the completed sales record sheet and answer the following:

1   What is the key market segment(s) for Car Mart?
2   List the particular features of this or these segment(s).
3   Describe which products and benefits best meet the needs of this segment(s).
4   Suggest ways that Car Mart could exploit this information to become a more successful business.
5   Is Car Mart the best name for this company? How might it be changed to communicate more accurately its type of business or the customers it serves?
6   Consider the main learning points from Car Mart and decide how you could apply them to your own company.

You might find it useful to make notes of any interesting issues that come out of this analysis in the space below, or on a separate sheet of paper. Once you have completed those questions, proceed to next section.

Notes

THE CUSTOMER AUDIT APPLIED TO YOUR OWN COMPANY

Working alone, and using your own company as the study vehicle:

1 Choose a major product or service, and identify

   (*a*) The main customers.
   (*b*) The features with maximum customer appeal.
   (*c*) The benefits to the customer of each feature.
   (*d*) Which of these benefits are differential benefits, i.e. are benefits not recognized or stressed by your major competitors.

2 If you cannot identify any differential benefits, in what ways could you develop them?
3 For those you have identified, how could they be improved upon?
4 Identify your key market segments. How do you describe them?
5 If you cannot readily identify any distinct segments, what would be a sensible way to segment your markets?

Personal notes

INTERPRETATION OF EXERCISE 4.5 – RATIONALE BEHIND CAR MART

1   The twelve customer cards represent two of each of the
    socioeconomic groups referred to in the supplementary material
    'Social Grading on National Research Surveys', p. 59 :

   Grade A   Chairman of industrial group.
             Senior partner in firm of solicitors.
   Grade B   Bank manager.
             Sales manager.
   Grade C_1 Teacher.
             Computer programmer.
   Grade C_2 Tool-maker.
             Plumber.
   Grade D   Bricklayer.
             Machine operator.
   Grade E   Lift attendant (normally a reserved occupation for the
             disabled)
             Elderly grannie.

2   The mechanism of using two dice in the way described means that,
    over about twenty transactions, something approaching Pareto's
    Law, comes into play, i.e. that 20 per cent of customers account
    for 80 per cent of sales. This is because card 1 is never chosen
    and cards in positions 6, 7 and 8 should be prominent. But since
    the layout of the cards is random, there can be no preconceived
    notions about customers – it must all be interpreted from the sales
    analysis.

3   There are some hidden learning objectives, because, by playing the
    game, people become aware of, and can distinguish:

   (*a*) Socioeconomic groupings.
   (*b*) Differences between features and benefits.
   (*c*) Differences between rational and psychological buying motives.

4   Car Mart provides enough data for anyone to bring to life the main
    points about customer analysis and segmentation.

5   Those who need to apply this learning to their own company
    situation will be able to proceed with more confidence.

6   Car Mart demands that there is a high level of focus on customers
    and ensures that there is high awareness of customer needs.

Supplementary material

1 CUSTOMER CLASSIFICATION SYSTEMS

(a) From 'Social Grading on National Research Surveys', JICNARS, 1978, Donald Monk, Extract from *Interviewers' Guide on Social Grading*

GUIDE TO GRADE 'A' HOUSEHOLDS UPPER MIDDLE CLASS
Informants from Grade 'A' households constitute about 3% of the total. The head of the household is a successful business or professional man, senior civil servant, or has considerable private means. A young man in some of these occupations who has not fully established himself may still be found in Grade 'B' though he eventually should reach Grade 'A'.

In country or suburban areas, 'A' grade households usually live in large detached houses or in expensive flats. In towns, they may live in expensive flats or town houses in the better parts of town. Some examples, which are by no means exhaustive, are given below.

Examples of occupations of the head of the household

Professional and semi-professional

Church of England dignitaries (bishop and above) and those of other denominations.
Physician, surgeon, specialist.
Established doctor, dentist (if a principal or partner in a large practice).
Established solicitor, barrister (own practice or partner in a large practice).
Matron of a large teaching hospital.
Headmaster of a public or grammar school or of any *large* school or college (i.e. 750 pupils or more).
Architect, chartered accountant, surveyor, actuary – fully qualified and principal or partner in a large practice. Also if working as a very senior (at or near board level) executive in a very large (200+) organization.
Senior civil servant, e.g. Permanent Secretary, Deputy Secretary, Under Secretary, Assistant Secretary, Principal.
Local Government chief officers.
Senior Local Government Officer (e.g. Town Clerk, Treasurer, County Planning Officer, Borough Surveyor).
University Professor.
Editor of a newspaper or magazine; senior journalist on national or very large provincial publication.
Commercial airline pilot (captain or first officer).
Captain of large merchant vessel (5,000 tons or more and/or 25+ crew).
Senior professional executives, i.e. professionally qualified people working as very senior executives or administrators (at or near board level in very large (200+) establishments) – e.g. Chief Engineer, Company Surveyor, Company Secretary, Chief Accountant, Curator, Artistic Director, Chief Designer, etc.
Librarian, qualified, in charge of a really major library.

Business and industry

Senior Buyers for leading wholesale or retail establishments.
Self-employed owners of businesses with 25 or more employees.
Self-employed farmers with 10 or more employees.
Board (i.e. Directors) or near board level Managers in large organizations (i.e. with 200 or more employees).
Managers in sole charge of branches or outlying establishments with 200 or more employees at the branch (e.g. factory managers, managers of very large retail establishments, depots, hotels, etc.).
Stock broker or jobber (principal or partner in the firm).
Insurance underwriter.
Advertising, research, public relations executives (and others offering professional or semi-professional services in specialized agencies) if at board level or principals or partners in agencies or practices with 25 or more employees.
Bank branch managers; managers of branches of other financial institutions (e.g. building society, insurance company, finance house) with 25 or more employees at the branch.

Police and Fire Brigade

Superintendent, Chief Constable.
C.I.D. Superintendent and Chief Superintendent.
Chief Fire Officer.

Armed Forces

Army – Lieut. Col. and above.
Navy – Commander and above.
RAF – Wing Commander and above.

Non-earners

People living in comfort on investments or private income.
Retired people where the head of the household before retirement would have been 'A' grade.

GUIDE TO GRADE 'B' HOUSEHOLDS
MIDDLE CLASS

Grade 'B' informants account for about 12% of the total. In general, the heads of 'B' Grade households will be quite senior people but not at the very top of their profession or business. They are quite well-off, but their style of life is generally respectable rather than rich or luxurious. Non-earners will be living on private pensions or on fairly modest private means.

Examples of occupations of the head of the household

Professional and semi-professional

Vicars, rectors, parsons, parish priests and ministers: clergymen above these ranks but below Bishop.

Headteachers of secondary, primary or preparatory schools with fewer than 750 pupils; qualified teachers aged 28 and over in public, secondary or grammar schools.

Civil servant – higher and senior and chief executive officers, executive officers. Recently-qualified assistant principal.

Local government – senior officers (9 grades).

University lecturers, readers; technical college lecturers.

Established journalist for provincial and local papers, trade and technical publications; less senior journalist for national press.

Matron of a smaller hospital (non-teaching); sister tutor in large hospital or teaching hospital.

Qualified pharmacist.

Qualified accountants, surveyors, architects, solicitors, etc., who do not have their own practices but are employed as executives not senior enough to be graded 'A'.

Newly qualified professional men of all sorts who have not yet established themselves (i.e. less than 3 years from qualification).

Librarian, qualified, in charge of a library or branch library.

Business and Industry

Self-employed owners of business with 5–24 employees in skilled or non-manual trades (e.g. shopkeepers, plumbing contractors, electrical contractors, etc.).

Self-employed farmers with 2–9 employees.

Managers of large farms, stewards, bailiffs, etc.

Bank clerks with special responsibilities (e.g. Chief clerk, teller, etc.)

Insurance clerk with professional qualifications and/or special responsibilities in large branch or head office.

Manager of a retail or wholesale establishment with 25–199 employees at the establishment.

Some relatively senior managers or executives in commerce and industry.

General Foreman, Clerk of Works, i.e. with other foremen under him.

Chief buyers for wholesale or retail establishments.

Area Sales Managers or senior representatives (especially if technically professionally qualified).

Executives with professional or technical qualifications who are not senior enough to be graded 'A', e.g. department managers.

Technicians with degree or equivalent qualifications, especially in high-technology industries such as electronics, computers, aircraft, chemicals, nuclear energy, etc.

Police and Fire Brigade

Chief Inspector, Inspector.
Assistant Chief Officer.
Divisional Officer.

Armed Forces

Army – Captain, Major.
Navy – Lieutenant, Lieutenant-Commander.
   R.A.F. – Flight Lieutenant. Squadron Leader.

Non-Earners

People with private income living in a less luxurious way than 'A' grade people. Retired people who, before retirement, would have been 'B' grade.

GUIDE TO GRADE 'C1' HOUSEHOLDS
LOWER MIDDLE CLASS

Grade 'C1' constitutes about 23% of total informants. In general it is made up of the families of small trades-people and non-manual workers who carry out less important administrative, supervisory and clerical jobs, i.e. what are sometimes called 'white-collar' workers.

Examples of occupations of the head of the household.

Professional and semi-professional

Curates in the Church of England: ministers of 'fringe' free churches; monks and nuns of any denomination, except those with special responsibilities.
Teachers, other than those graded 'B'.
Student nurses; staff nurses; sisters in smaller hospitals; Midwife; Dispenser; Radiographer.
Bank clerk, insurance clerk with no special qualifications or responsibilities.
Insurance agent (door to door collector).
Civil Servant – clerical grades.
Local government – clerical, junior administrative, professional and technical grades.
Articled clerk.
Library assistant (not fully qualified).
Student (on grant).

Business and Industry

Self-employed owners of small business (with 1–4 employees) in non-manual or skilled trades, e.g. shopkeepers, electrical contractors, builders, etc.
Self-employed farmers with only one employee.
Manager of a retail or wholesale establishment with 1–24 employees.
Some relatively junior managers in industry and commerce.
Clerks, typists, office machine operators, punch operators.
Telephonists, telegraphists.
Buyers (except very senior buyers).
Representatives, salesmen (except those graded 'B').
Technicians/Engineers, etc. with professional/technical qualifications below degree standard.

Foremen in charge of 25 or more employees, mainly supervisory work (other than a few very senior foremen coded 'B').
Draughtsman.
Driving instructor.

Police and Fire Brigade

Station Sergeant, Sergeant, Detective Sergeant.
Station Officer & Sub-Station Officer, Leading Fireman.

Armed Forces

Army – Sergeant, Sergeant Major, Warrant Officer, 2nd Lieutenant, Lieutenant.
Navy – Petty Officer, Chief Petty Officer, Sub-Lieutenant.
R.A.F. – Sergeant, Flight Sergeant, Warrant Officer, Pilot Officer, Flying Officer.

Non-Earners

Retired people who, before retirement, would have been C1 grade and have pensions other than state pensions or have private means of a very modest nature.

GUIDE TO GRADE 'C2' HOUSEHOLDS
THE SKILLED WORKING CLASS

Grade C2 consists in the main of skilled manual workers and their families. It constitutes about 32% of informants. When in doubt as to whether the head of the household is skilled or unskilled, check whether he has served an apprenticeship; this may be a guide, though not all skilled workers have served an apprenticeship.

Examples of occupations of the head of the household

General

Foreman (responsible for up to 24 employees), Deputy (mining) Charge Hand, Overlooker, Overseer, whose work is mainly manual (these may be found in nearly all trades and industries – including farming and agriculture).

Agriculture

Agricultural workers with special skill or responsibilities, e.g. head cowman, shepherd (chief).

Building Industry (including Construction and Woodworkers).

Most adult male skilled workers or craftsmen including: Bricklayer, Carpenter, Plasterer, Glazier, Plumber, Painter.

Coal Mining

Skilled underground workers, including: Coal Cutter, Filler, Getter, Hewer, Miner, Putter.

Metal Manufacturing, Shipbuilding and Repairing, Engineering, Furnace, Forge, Foundry and Rolling Mills.

Most adult male workers including: Furnaceman (except coal, gas and coke ovens), Moulder, Smelter, Blacksmith, Coppersmith.
Plater, Riveter, Shipwright.
Fitter, Grinder, Millwright, Setter, Toolmaker, Turner.
Vehicle Builder, Welder.
Electrical Fitter, Electrician, Lineman.
Skilled Labourer (docks and Admiralty only).

Rubber

Most adult skilled workers.

Textiles, Clothing and Leather

Skilled workers in rayon or nylon production.
Skilled Knitters (hoisery or other knitted goods). Weaver, Bleacher, Dryer, Drawer-in.
Boot and Shoemaker.
Cutter and Fitter – Tailoring.

Furniture and Upholstery

Most adult male skilled workers including the following:
Carpenter, Joiner, Cabinet Maker.

Paper and Printing Trades

Most adult male skilled workers, including:
Machine Man, Finisher (paper and board manufacturer).
Compositor, Linotype Operator, Typesetter, Electrotyper, Sterotyper, Process Engraver.

Transport

A few only of the better paid workers such as:
All heavy and long distance Vehicle drivers, Engine Driver and Fireman.
Bus Drivers, Bus Inspectors, Signalmen, Train Drivers, Shunters.
Passenger and Goods Guards.
A.A. Patrolman, Ambulance Drivers.
Post Office Sorters and high grade Postmen.
Stevedore.

Distributive trades

Proprietors and Managers of small shops with no employees.
Shop Assistants with responsibilities.

Glass and Ceramics

Most adult workers including:
Formers, Finishers and Decorators, Furnacemen and Kilnmen.

Electrical and Electronics

Including Radio and Radar Mechanics, Telephone installers and Linesmen, Electrical and
Electronic Fitters.

Agriculture – Farming, Forestry and Fishing

Skilled and specialized workers.

Food and drink

Baker.
Pastrycook.
Brewer.
  Maltster.

Police and Fire Brigade

Prison Officer.
Constable.
Fireman.
  C.I.D. Detective Constable.

Security Officers – (Securicor)

Miscellaneous

Self-employed unskilled manual workers with 1–4 employees. e.g. Chimney Sweep, Window Cleaner, Taxi Driver (London).
Self-employed skilled manual workers with no employees.
Coach Builder, Plumber.
  Dental Mechanic and Technician.

Armed Forces

Army – Lance Corporal, Corporal.
Navy – A.B. Seaman, Leading Seaman
  R.A.F. – Aircraftsman, Leading and Senior.

Non-earners

Retired people who before retirement would have been in C2 grade and have pensions other than State Pensions or have private means.

GUIDE TO GRADE 'D' HOUSEHOLDS
THE SEMI-SKILLED AND UNSKILLED WORKING CLASS

Grade D consists entirely of manual workers, generally semi-skilled or unskilled. This grade accounts for 21% of families.

Examples of occupations of the head of the household.

General

Most semi-skilled and unskilled workers.
Labourers and mates of the occupations included in C2 grade.
All apprentices to skilled trades.

Agriculture – Farming, Forestry and Fishing

The majority of male agricultural workers, other than those with special skills or responsibilities, including:
Tractor or other agricultural machine Driver, Ditcher, Hedger, Farm Labourer.
Forestry Worker, Timber Man.
Fisherman.
  Gardeners and Self-employed Market Gardeners with no employees.

Coal Mining and Quarrying

Surface workers except those with special responsibilities.
Unskilled underground workers.

Textiles and Clothing Manufacture

Most manual workers including the following:
Woolsorter, Blender, Carder, Comber, Spinner, Doubler, Twister, Textile Printer.
   Machinist (clothing manufacturer).

Food, Drink and Tobacco

The majority of adult workers, including the following:
Dough Mixer, Oven Man.
Bottler, Opener.
   Stripper, Cutter (Tobacco).

Transport

Bus Conductor, Railway Porter including Leading Porter.
Ticket Collector (Railway).
Cleaner.
   Traffic Warden.

Distributive Trades

Shop assistant without special training or responsibility.

Gas, Coke and Chemical

Most adult workers including Furnacemen and chemical production process workers.

Plastics

Most adult workers.

Glass and Ceramics

Production process workers.

Electrical and Electronics

Assemblers.

Miscellaneous

Caretaker, Warehouseman, Park Keeper, Storekeeper, Postman, Works Policeman, Domestic Servant, Woman Factory Worker, Waitress, Laundry Worker.

All goods delivery including milk and bread roundsmen.
Meter Readers.
Self-employed unskilled manual workers with no employees, e.g. Window Cleaner, Chimney Sweep, Taxi Driver (provinces).

Armed Forces

Army – Private or equivalent.
Navy – Ordinary Seaman.
   R.A.F. – Aircraftsman.

Non-earners

Retired people who before retirement would have been in D grade and have pensions other than State Pensions, or have other private means.

GUIDE TO GRADE 'E' HOUSEHOLDS
THOSE AT LOWEST LEVELS OF SUBSISTENCE

Grade E consists of Old Age Pensioners, Widows and their families, casual workers and those who, through sickness or unemployment, are dependent on social security schemes, or have very small private means. They constitute about 9% of all informants. Individual income of the head of the household (disregarding additions such as supplementary benefits) will be little, if any, above the basic flat-rate social security benefit.

Examples of occupations of the head of the household.

Earners

Casual Labourers.
Part-time clerical and other workers.

Non-earners

Old Age Pensioners.
Widow (with State Widow's Pension).
Those dependent on sickness, unemployment and supplementary benefits for over 2 months who are without benefits related to earnings.
Disabled Pensioners.
Private means, Private pension, disability pension compensation, etc. amounting to little, if any, above the basic flat-rate social security benefit.

Only those informants will be graded as E whose head of the households is E and where no other member of the family is in fact the Chief Wage Earner.

EXAMPLES OF OCCUPATIONS UNDER INDUSTRIES

Social Grade

I Farmers, Foresters, Fishermen

D	Agricultural workers, unskilled.
C2	Skilled agricultural workers.
D	Agricultural machinery drivers.
D	Gardeners with no
D	Foresters and woodmen qualifications.
D	Fishermen (employed).
C1	Agricultural workers – junior technically qualified.
B	Grieve (Scotland only) farm manager, bailiff, steward (of large farms or estates).

II Miners and Quarrymen

C2	Coal mine – face workers.
C2	Coal mine – underground workers (skilled).
D	Coal mine – underground workers (unskilled).
D	Coal miners (majority of workers above ground).

III Gas, Coke and Chemicals Makers

D	Furnacemen, coal, gas and coke ovens.
D	Chemical production process workers.

IV Glass and Ceramics Makers

C2	Ceramic formers.
C2	Glass formers, finishers and decorators.
C2	Furnacemen, kilnmen, glass and ceramic.
C2	Ceramics' decorators and finishers.
C2	Ceramics' decorators doing hand painting.
D	Glass and ceramics production process workers.

V Furnace, Forge, Foundry, Rolling Mill Workers

C2	Furnacemen – metal.
C2	Rolling, tube mill operators, metal drawers.
C2	Moulders and coremakers (foundry).
C2	Smiths, forgemen.
D	Metal making and treating workers.
D	Fettlers, metal dressers.

VI Electrical and Electronic Workers

C2	Radio and radar mechanics.
C2	Installers and repairmen, telephone.
C2	Linesmen, cable jointers.
C2	Electricians.
C2	Electrical and electronic fitters.
D	Assemblers (electrical and electronic).
C2	Electrical engineers (manual).
D	Mates to above workers.

VII Engineering and Allied Trades Workers

C2	Sheet Metal workers.
C2	Constructional engineers: riggers.
C2	Metal plate workers: riveters.
C2	Gas, electric welders, cutters: braziers.
C2	Machine tool setters, setter-operators.
D	Machine tool operators.
C2	Tool makers, tool room fitters.
C2	Fitters, machine erectors, etc.
C2	Engineers (manual).
C2	Electro-platers, dip platers and related workers.
C2	Plumbers, lead burners, pipe fitters.
D	Press workers and stampers.
C2	Metal workers (skilled).
C2	Watch and chronometer makers and repairers.
C2	Precision instrument makers and repairers.
C2	Goldsmiths, silversmiths, jewellery makers.
C2	Coach, carriage, wagon builders and repairers.
D	Other metal making, working; jewellery and electrical production process workers (unskilled).

VIII Woodworkers

C2	Carpenters and joiners.
C2	Cabinet makers.
C2	Sawyers and wood working machinists.
C2	Coopers, hoop makers and benders.
C2	Pattern makers.
C2	Woodworkers.
D	Mates to above workers.

IX Leather Workers

C2	Tanners: leather, fur dressers, fellmongers.
C2	Shoemakers.
C2	Shoe repairers.
C2	Cutters, lasters, sewers, footwear and related workers.
C2	Leather product makers.
D	Mates to above workers.

X Textile Workers

D	Fibre preparers.
D	Spinners, doublers, winders, reelers.
C2	Warpers, sizers.
C2	Drawers-in.
C2	Weavers.
D	Weavers – jute, flax, hemp (Scotland only).
C2	Knitters.
C2	Bleachers and finishers of textiles.
C2	Dyers of textiles.
C2	Textile fabrics and related product makers and examiners.
D	Textile fabrics etc., production process workers.

D Winders and reelers.
C2 Rope, twine and net makers.

XI Clothing Workers

C2 Tailors – cutters and fitters.
C2 Upholsterers and related workers.
D Sewers and embroiderers, textile and light leather products.

XII Food, Drink and Tobacco Workers

C2 Bakers and pastry cooks.
C2 Butchers and meat cutters.
C2 Brewers, wine makers and related workers.
D Food processors.
D Tobacco preparers and product makers.

XIII Paper and Printing Workers

C2 Makers of paper and paperboard.
C2 Paper products makers.
C2 Compositors.
C2 Printing press operators.
C2 Printers (so described).
C2 Printing workers.
D Mates to above workers.

XIV Makers of Other Products

C2 Workers in rubber.
D Workers in plastics.
C2 Craftsmen.
D Other production process workers.
D Mates to above workers.

XV Construction Workers

C2 Bricklayers, tile setters.
C2 Masons, stone cutters, slate workers.
C2 Plasterers, cement finishers, terrazzo workers.
D Mates to above workers.

XVI Painters and Decorators

D Aerographers, paint sprayers.
C2 Painters, decorators.
D Mates to above workers.

XVII Drivers of Stationary Engines, Cranes etc.

D Boiler firemen.
C2 Crane and hoist operators: slingers.
C2 Operators of earth moving and other construction machinery.
D Stationary engine, materials handling plant operators: oilers and greasers.

XVIII   Labourers

D	Railway lengthmen.
D	Labourers and unskilled workers.
D	Chemical and allied trades.
D	Engineering and allied trades.
D	Foundries in engineering and allied trades.
D	Textiles.
D	Coke ovens and gas works.
D	Glass and ceramics.
D	Building and contracting.
D	All other labourers.

XIX   Transport and Communications Workers

B	Deck, engineering officers and pilots, ship.
D	Deck and engine room rating, barge and boatmen.
A	Aircraft pilots, navigators and flight engineers.
C2	Drivers, motormen, firemen, railway engine.
C2	Railway guards (passenger and goods).
C2	Drivers of buses, coaches, trams.
C2	Drivers of road goods vehicles – heavy or long distance.
D	Drivers of road goods vehicles – local and light.
C2	Shunters, pointmen.
C1	Telephone operators.
C1	Telegraph and radio operators.
D	Postmen.
C2	Sorters and higher grade postmen.
D	Messengers.
D	Bus and tram conductors.
D	Porters, railway.
D	Ticket collectors, railway.
C2	Bus Inspector.
C2	Stevedores.
D	Dock labourers.
C2	Skilled labourer (Docks & Admiralty only).
D	Lorry drivers' mates, van guards.
D	Unskilled workers in transport and communication occupations.

XX   Warehousemen, Storekeepers, Packers, Bottlers

D	Warehousemen, storekeepers.
D	Assistant warehousemen, assistant storekeepers.
D	Packers, labellers and related workers.

XXI   Clerical Workers

C1	Typists.
C1	Shorthand writers, secretaries.
C1	Clerks, cashiers, office machine operators.

XXII   Sales Workers

C1	Salesmen, representatives (unless professionally qualified).
C1	Shop assistants with qualifications and training.

C2	Shop assistants with special responsibilities.
D	Shop assistants without special responsibilities and training.
D	Roundsmen (bread, milk, laundry, soft drinks).
D	Street vendors, hawkers.

XXIII   Service, Sport and Recreation Workers

C2	Security guards.
D	Barmen, barmaids.
D	Housekeepers.
D	Stewards.
D	Waiters, counter hands.
C2	Cooks.
D	Kitchen hands.
D	Maids, valets and related service workers.
D	Caretakers, office keepers.
D	Chimney sweeps (employed).
D	Charwomen, office cleaners.
D	Window cleaners (employed).
C2	Hairdressers, beauticians if apprenticeship served.
D	Hairdressers, beauticians if serving apprenticeship.
D	Hospital or ward orderlies.
D	Launderers, dry cleaners and pressers.
C2	Ambulance men.

XXIV   Administrators and Managers

| A | Ministers of the Crown; M.P.s: senior Government Officials. |
| A | Local authority senior officers. |

XXV   Professional, Technical Workers, Artists

A	Medical practitioners (qualified with own practice).
B	Junior medical practitioners (recently qualified).
A	Dental practitioners (qualified with own practice).
B	Junior practitioners.
	Authors, journalists and related workers.
A,B,C1	Stage managers, actors, entertainers, musicians.
	Painters, sculptors and related creative artists.

The grade of these and similar cases, e.g. sportsmen obviously depends on their success and your grading must depend upon this.

(b) THE HALL-JONES CLASSIFICATION OF OCCUPATIONS
From J. Goldthorpe *et. al.*, *The Affluent Worker: Industrial Attitudes and Behaviour.* Cambridge UP, 1968.

The occupational classification set out below *was constructed on the basis of previous efforts by British sociologists, notably that of Hall and Caradog Jones.*

   In allocating occupations to classes we followed the general rule of choosing the 'lower' alternative in all bordering cases or cases where our information was incomplete or ambiguous. The examples given below are selected in order to give some idea of the range of occupation included in particular categories as well as of 'typical' occupations.

Occupational Status Level	*Example*	*R.G.'s Social class equivalent*
1(a) Higher professional, managerial and other white-collar employees.	Chartered accountant, business executive, senior civil servant, graduate teacher.	I
(b) Large industrial or commercial employers, landed proprietors.	–	
2(a) Intermediate professional, managerial and other white-collar employees.	Pharmacist, non-graduate teacher, departmental manager, bank cashier.	II
(b) Medium industrial or commercial employers, substantial farmers.	–	
3(a) Lower professional, managerial and other white-collar employees.	Chiropodist, bar manager, commercial traveller, draughtsman, accounts or wages clerk.	III non-man
(b) Small industrial or commercial employers, small farmers.	Jobbing builder, taxi owner-driver, tobacconist.	
4(a) Supervisory, inspectional, minor official and service employees.	Foreman, meter-reader, shop assistant, door-to-door salesman.	III Man or non-man
(b) Self-employed men (no employees or expensive capital equipment).	Window cleaner, jobbing gardener.	
5 Skilled manual workers (with apprenticeship or equivalent).	–	III
6 Other relatively skilled manual workers	Unapprenticed mechanics and fitters, skilled miners, painters and decorators, p.s.v. drivers.	III MAN or IV
7 Semi-skilled manual workers	Machine operator, assembler, storeman.	IV
8 Unskilled manual workers	Farm labourer, builder's labourer, dustmen.	V

(c) **AN OVERVIEW OF THE LIFE CYCLE,** from 'Life Cycle Concept in Marketing Research', George Gubar & William D. Wells, *Journal of Marketing Research*, November 1966.

Bachelor stage, young single people not living at home	*New'y married couples, young, no children*	*Full nest I, youngest child under six*	*Full nest II, youngest child six or over six*
Few financial burdens	Better off financially than they will be in the near future	Home purchases at peak, liquid assets low	Financial position better
Fashion opinion leaders			Some wives work
Recreation orientation	Highest purchase rate & highest average purchase of durables	Dissatisfied with financial position & amount of money saved	Less influenced by advertising
BUY: basic kitchen equipment, basic furniture, cars, equipment for the mating game, vacation	BUY: cars, refrigerators, stoves, sensible & durable furnit ure, vacations	Interested in new products	Buy larger sized packages, multi-unit deals
		Like advertised products	BUY: many foods, cleaning materials, bicycles, music lessons, pianos
		BUY: washers, dryers, TV, baby food, chest rubs & cough medicine, vitamins, dolls, wagons, skates	

Full nest III, older married couples with dependent children	*Empty Nest I, older married couples, no children living with them, head of labour force*	*Empty Nest II, older married couples, no children living at home, head retired*	*Solitary survivor, in labour force*	*Solitary survivor, retired*
Financial position still better	Home ownership at peak	Drastic cut in income	Income still good but likely to sell home	Some medical & products needs as other retired group, drastic cut in income
More wives work	Most satisfied with financial position	Keep home		
Some children get jobs	& money saved	BUY: medical appliances, medical care, products which aid health, sleep & digestion		Special need for attention, affection & security
Hard to influence with advertising	Interested in travel, recrea-tion, self education			
High average purchase of durables	Make gifts & contributions			
BUY: new more tasteful furniture, autotravel, non-necessary appliances, boats, dental services, magazines	Not interestedin new products			
	BUY: vacations, luxuries, home improvements			

(*d*) REGISTRAR-GENERAL'S 'SOCIAL CLASS'

Occupied and Retired Males aged 15 and over		*% of Total*		
	1931	*1951*	*1961*	*1971*[1]
	2	3	4	5

Class I: Professional, Administrative
Examples: Company Directors & Secretaries, Bankers, Shipowners & Managers, Stockbrokers, Insurance Underwriters, Clergymen, Lawyers, Doctors, Scientists, Admin. class of civil service, officers of armed forces. Professional engineers (Civil, electrical etc.)

Class II: Intermediate 13 14 15 17
Owners & Managers: Farmers, land agents, dock and harbour officials, local authority, admin., Commercial managers, hotel managers, proprietors of retail shops.
   Professional: Teachers, trained nurses, medical auxiliaries, social welfare workers, artists, civil service executive class.

Class III: Skilled Workers 49 52 51 48[2]
Four main sub-groups: (a) foreman, under managers (M=11
& overlookers. (b) clerks, typists. (c) skilled craftsmen. N=37)
(d) salesmen, shop assistants.

Class IV: Intermediate 18 16 21 17
Semi-skilled machine minders, labourers assisting craftsmen provided there is some degree of skill.

Class V: Unskilled Labour 18 15 9 8
Railway porters, builders's labourers, dock labourers, lift attendants, watchmen, charwomen.

NB. For the 1961 Census the following main alterations were made:

(a) University teachers from Class 2 to Class 1
(b) Administrative Civil servants from Class 1 to Class 2
(c) Actors and musicians from Class 3 to Class 2
(d) Postmen and telephone operators from Class 3 to Class 4

1 1981 Census not yet published.
2 For 1980 'Social Class' changes, see list below.

REGISTRAR-GENERAL'S 'SOCIAL CLASS'

Class I Professional occupations

General administrators – national government (Assistant Secretary and above). Judges, Solicitors, Accountants, Management Consultants, Clergymen, Doctors, Dentists, Opticians, Vets., Scientists, Engineers, Architects, Town Planners, Mathematicians.

Class II Intermediate occupations

Personnel and Industrial Relations Officers, Authors, Marketing, Advertising, P.R. executives, Sales Managers, Actors, Entertainers, Proprietors and Managers of Hotels, pubs etc., Company Secretaries, Brokers, Taxation experts, Computer programmers. Teachers, Nurses, Farmers, Police Officers (inspectors and above), Prison Officers (Chief Officers and above). National government (H.E.O. to Senior Principal level). Local government officers (administration and executive functions.)

Class III (N) Skilled occupations-Non-manual

Market and Street Traders, Typists, Secretaries, Driving Instructors, Hairdressers and Barbers, Managers and Proprietors, Restaurateurs, Sales Reps., Scrap Dealers, Supervisors of: clerks, telephone operators, tracers, shop assistants, Police Sergeants.

Class III (M) Skilled occupations – Manual

Repairers – shoes, watches, t.v., radio; Production workers for various industries, plumbers, welders, fitter/mechanics, painters, building workers, gardeners, service workers, Foremen/Supervisors, Bus Inspectors.

Class IV Partly skilled occupations

Street traders and assistants, Security Guards, Materials processing handlers. Sewers, making and repairing of – plastics, other (excluding metal and electrical), machine tool operators, construction workers, Waiters/waitresses, Bar staff, domestic assistants, bus conductors.

Class V Unskilled occupations

Messengers, dustmen, cleaners, drivers mates, stevedores, dockers, Railway stationmen, Labourers and unskilled workers in textiles, gas works, chemicals etc.

Source: Classification of Occupations 1989. Office of Population, Census and Surveys.

2 STANDARD INDUSTRIAL CLASSIFICATION

A000 AGRICULTURE, FORESTRY AND FISHING

	A100	Agriculture and Horticulture
	A200	Forestry
	A300	Fishing

1000 ENERGY AND WATER SUPPLY INDUSTRIES

	1100	Coal Extraction and Manufacture of Solid Fuels
	1113	Deep Coal Mines
	1114	Open Coal Working
	1115	Manufacture of Solid Fuels
	1200	Coke Ovens
	1300	Extraction of Mineral Oil and Natural Gas
	1400	Mineral Oil Processing
	14A1	Mineral Oil Refining
	14A2	Other Treatment of Petroleum Products
	1500	Nuclear Fuel Production
	1600	Production & Distribution of Electricity, Gas & Other Forms of Energy
	1610	Production & Distribution of Electricity
	1620	Public Gas Supply

2567	Miscellaneous Chemical Products for Industrial Use
2568	Formulated Pesticides
2569	Adhesive Film, Cloth and Foil
2570	Pharmaceutical Products
2580	Soap & Toilet Preparations
2581	Soap & Synthetic Detergents
2582	Perfumes, Cosmetics and Toilet Preparations
2590	Specialized Chemical Products Mainly for Household and Office Use
2591	Photographic Materials and Chemicals
2599	Chemical Products, Not Elsewhere Specified
2600	Production of Man-Made Fibres

3000 METAL GOODS, ENGINEERING AND VEHICLE INDUSTRIES

3100	Manufacture of Metal Goods Not Elsewhere Specified
3111	Ferrous Metal Foundries
3112	Non-Ferrous Metal Foundries
3120	Forging, Pressing and Stamping
3130	Bolts, Nuts etc. Springs: Non-Precision Chains: Metals Treatment
3137	Bolts, Nuts, Washers, Rivets, Springs & Non-Precision Chains
3138	Heat and Surface Treatment of Metals, Including Sintering
3142	Metal Doors, Windows etc.
3160	Hand Tools and Finished Metal Goods
3161	Hand Tools and Implements
3162	Cutlery, Spoons, Forks and Similar Tableware: Razors
3163	Metal Storage Vessels (Mainly Non-Industrial)
3164	Packaging Products of Metal (Cans & Boxes)
3165	Domestic Heating and Cooking Appliances (Non-Electrical)
3166	Metal Furniture and Safes
3167	Domestic & Similar Utensils of Metal
3169	Finished Metal Products, Needles, Pins, Smallwares, Mountings for Furniture
3200	Mechanical Engineering
32A0	Industrial Plant & Steelwork
32A4	Fabricated Constructional Steelwork
32A5	Boilers and Process Plant Fabrications
3210	Agricultural Machinery and Tractors
3211	Agricultural Machinery
3212	Wheeled Tractors
3220	Metal-Working Machine Tools and Engineers Tools
3221	Metal-Working Machine Tools
3222	Engineers' Small Tools
3230	Textile Machinery
3240	Machinery for the Food, Chemical and Related Industries
3244	Food, Drink and Tobacco Processing Machinery: Packaging and Bottling Machinery
3245	Chemical Industry Machinery: Furnaces & Kilns; Gas, Water and Waste Treatment Plant
324A	Chemical Industry Machinery
324B	Furnaces & Kilns
324C	Gas, Water & Waste Treatment Plant
3246	Process Engineering Contractors
3250	Mining Machinery, Construction and Mechanical Handling Equipment
3251	Mining Machinery

3254	Construction and Earth Moving Equipment
3255	Mechanical Lifting and Handling Equipment
3260	Mechanical Power Transmission Equipment
3261	Precision Chains
3262	Ball, Needle & Roller Bearings
3270	Machinery for Printing, Paper, Wood, Leather, Rubber, Glass and Related Industries; Laundry and Dry Cleaning Machinery
3275	Machinery for Wood, Leather, Rubber, Glass & Related Industries; Laundry & Dry Cleaning Machinery
327A	Woodworking Machinery
327B	Rubber and Plastics Working Machinery
327C	Leather Working and Footwear Making and Repairing Machinery
327D	Paper Making Machinery
327E	Glass and Brick Making and Similar Machinery
327F	Laundry and Dry Cleaning Machinery
3276	Printing, Bookbinding and Paper Goods Machinery
3280	Other Machinery and Mechanical Equipment
3281	Internal Combustion Engines
3283	Compressors and Fluid Power Equipment
3284	Refrigerating Machinery, Space Heating, Ventilating and Air Conditioning Equipment
3285	Scales, Weighing Machinery and Portable Power Tools
3286	Other Industrial & Commercial Machinery
3287	Pumps
3288	Industrial Valves
3289	Mechanical, Marine and Precision Engineering not Elsewhere Specified
3290	Ordnance, Small Arms and Ammunition
3300	Manufacture of Office Machinery and Data Processing Equipment
33A1	Office Machinery
33A2	Electronic Data Processing Equipment
3400	Electrical and Electronic Engineering
3410	Insulated Wires and Cables
3420	Basic Electrical Equipment
3430	Electrical Equipment for Industrial Use, and Batteries & Accumulators
3432	Batteries & Accumulators
3433	Alarms and Signalling Equipment
3434	Electrical Equipment for Motor Vehicles. Cycles & Aircraft
3435	Electrical Equipment for Industrial Use, Not Elsewhere Specified
3440	Telecommunications Equipment, Electrical Measuring Equipment, Electronic Capital Goods & Passive Electronic Components
3441	Telegraph and Telephone Apparatus & Equipment
3442	Electrical Instruments and Control Systems
3443	Radio and Electronic Capital Goods
3444	Components Other than Active Components Mainly for Electronic Equipment
3450	Other Electronic Equipment
3452	Gramophone Records and Pre-recorded Tapes
3453	Active Components and Electronic Sub-Assemblies
3454	Electronic Consumer Goods and Other Electronic Equipment, Not Elsewhere Specified
3460	Domestic-Type Electrical Appliances
3470	Electric Lamps and Other Electric Lighting Equipment
3480	Electrical Equipment Installation

3500	Manufacture of Motor Vehicles and Parts Thereof
3510	Motor Vehicles and their Engines
3520	Motor Vehicle Bodies, Trailers and Caravans
3521	Motor Vehicle Bodies
3522	Trailers and Semi-Trailers
3523	Caravans
3530	Motor Vehicle Parts
3600	Manufacture of Other Transport Equipment
3610	Shipbuilding and Repairing
3620	Railway & Tramway Vehicles
3630	Cycles and Motor Cycles
3633	Motor Cycles & Parts
3634	Pedal Cycles & Parts
3640	Aerospace Equipment Manufacturing and Repairing
3650	Other Vehicles
3700	Instrument Engineering
3710	Measuring, Checking and Precision Instruments and Apparatus
3720	Medical and Surgical Equipment and Orthopaedic Appliances
3730	Optical Precision Instruments and Photographic Equipment
3731	Spectacles and Unmounted Lenses
3732	Optical Precision Instruments
3733	Photographic & Cinematographic Equipment
3740	Clocks, Watches and Other Timing Devices

4000 OTHER MANUFACTURING INDUSTRIES

4100	Food, Drink & Tobacco Manufacturing Industries
4110	Organic, Oils and Fats (Other Than Crude Animal Fats)
4115	Margarine and Compound Cooking Fats
4116	Processing Organic Oils and Fats (Other than Crude Animal Fat Production)
4120	Slaughtering of Animals and Production of Meat & By-Products
4121	Slaughter Houses
4122	Bacon Curing and Meat Processing
4123	Poultry Slaughter and Processing
4126	Animal By-Product Processing
4130	Preparation of Milk & Milk Products
4140	Processing of Fruit and Vegetables
4150	Fish Processing
4160	Grain Milling
4180	Starch
4190	Bread, Biscuits and Flour Confectionery
4196	Bread and Flour Confectionery
4197	Biscuits and Crispbread
4200	Sugar and Sugar By-Products
4210	Ice Cream, Cocoa, Chocolate and Sugar Confectionery
4213	Ice Cream
4214	Cocoa, Chocolate and Sugar Confectionery
4220	Animal Feeding Stuffs
4221	Compound Animal Feeds
4222	Pet Foods and Non-Compound Animal Feeds
4230	Miscellaneous Foods
4240	Spirit Distilling and Compounding
4260	Wines, Cider and Perry

4270	Brewing and Malting
4280	Soft Drinks
4290	Tobacco Industry
4300	Textile Industry
4310	Woollen & Worsted Industry
4320	Cotton and Silk Industries
4321	Spinning and Doubling on the Cotton System
4322	Weaving of Cotton, Silk and Man-Made Fibres
4330	Throwing, Texturing etc. of Continuous Filament Yarn
4340	Spinning and Weaving Flax, Hemp and Ramie
4350	Jute and Polypropylene Yarns and Fabrics
4360	Hosiery and Other Knitted Goods
4363	Hosiery and Other Weft Goods and Fabrics
4364	Warp Knitted Goods
4370	Textile Finishing
4380	Carpets and Other Textile Floor Coverings
4384	Pile Carpets and Carpeting & Rugs (Woven-Tufted)
4385	Other Carpets, Carpeting, Rugs and Matting (Needles & Bonded Hard Fibre)
4390	Miscellaneous Textiles
4395	Lace
4396	Rope, Twine & Net
4398	Narrow Fabrics (Braided Elastics – Ribbons, Braids & Trimmings)
4399	Other Miscellaneous Textiles (Felt-Kapok & Vegetable Down)
4400	Manufacture of Leather & Leather Goods
4410	Leather and Fellmongery
4420	Leather Goods
4500	Footwear and Clothing Industries
4510	Footwear
4530	Clothing, Hats and Gloves
4531	Weatherproof Outer wear
4532	Men's and Boy's Tailored Outer Wear
4533	Women's and Girl's Tailored Outer Wear
4534	Working Clothing and Men's and Boy's Jeans
4535	Men's and Boy's Shirts, Underwear and Nightwear
4536	Women's and Girl's Light Outerwear, Lingerie and Infant's Wear
4537	Hats, Caps and Millinery
4538	Gloves
4539	Other Dress Industries
4550	Household Textiles and Other made up Textiles
4555	Soft Furnishings
4556	Canvas Goods, Sacks and Other made up Textiles
4557	Household Textiles
4560	Fur Goods
4600	Timber and Wooden Furniture Industries
4610	Sawmilling, Planing etc. of Wood
4620	Manufacture of Semi-Finished Wood Products and Treatment of Wood
4630	Builder's Carpentry and Joinery
4640	Wooden Containers
4650	Other Wooden Articles (Except Furniture)
4660	Articles of Cork and Plaiting Materials, Brushes and Brooms
4663	Brushes and Brooms
4664	Articles of Cork and Basket Ware, Wicker Work and Other Plaiting Materials

4670	Wooden and Upholstered Furniture & Shop & Office Fittings
4671	Wooden & Upholstered Furniture
4672	Shop and Office Fitting
4700	Manufacture of Paper and Paper Products: Printing & Publishing
4710	Pulp, Paper and Board (Pulp, Newsprint, Writing & Printing Papers, Wrapping & Packaging Papers, Household, Toilet Papers & Tissues, Industrial, Corrugated, Bituminized)
4720	Conversion of Paper and Board
4721	Wall Coverings
4722	Household and Personal Hygiene Products of Paper
4723	Stationery (Note Paper, Binders etc)
4724	Packaging Products of Paper & Pulp (Sacks and Bags, Other)
4725	Packaging Products of Board (Fibre Board Packing Cases, Rigid Boxes, Cartons)
4728	Other Paper & Board Products (Papier Mache or Wood Pulp not Elsewhere Specified)
4750	Printing & Publishing
4751	Printing & Publishing of Newspapers
4752	Printing & Publishing of Periodicals
4753	Printing & Publishing of Books
4754	Other Printing & Publishing (Security Printing e.g. Bank Notes, Stamps, Tickets, Greeting Cards; Bookbinding, Etching, Engraving, Printing on Metal)
4800	Processing of Rubber & Plastics
4810	Rubber Products
4811	Rubber Tyres & Inner Tubes
4812	Other Rubber Products-Hose & Tubing, Belting, Reclaimed Rubber
4820	Retreading & Specialist Repairing of Rubber Tyres
4830	Processing of Plastics
4831	Plastic Coated Textile Fabric
4832	Plastics Semi-Manufactures
4833	Plastics Floorcoverings
4834	Plastics Building Products
4835	Plastics Packaging Products
4836	Plastics Products not Elsewhere Specified
4900	Other Manufacturing Industries
4910	Jewellery and Coins
4920	Musical Instruments
4930	Photographic & Cinematographic Processing Laboratories
4940	Toys & Sports Goods
4941	Toys & Games
4942	Sports Goods
4950	Miscellaneous Manufacturing Industries
4954	Miscellaneous Stationers Goods (Pens & Pencils, Inks, Office Accessories)
4959	Other Manufacturers (Ivory, Meerschaum, Bone, Horn, Tortoise-shell & Smokers Requisites, Taxidermist)

5A00 CONSTRUCTION: General Construction & Demolition Work

5AAA	Property Developers
5AAB	Municipal & Service Building Contractors
5AAC	Concrete Work
5AAD	Structural Steel Work
5AAE	Excavation & Foundation Work
5AAF	Wreckage & Demolition

5A10	Construction and Repair of Buildings
5A1A	Domestic House Builders
5A1B	Residential Construction – Hotels, Flats, etc.
5A1C	Industrial Building Contractors
5A1D	Scaffolding Erection
5A20	Civil Engineering
5A2A	Street & Paving Construction
5A2B	Bridge, Tunnel & Flyover Construction
5A2C	Water, Sewer, Pipe Line & Power-Line Construction & Installation
5A2D	Heavy Construction & Civil Engineering
5A30	Installation of Fixtures & Fittings
5A3A	Plumbing, Heating & Air Conditioning
5A3B	Electrical Contracting
5A40	Building Completion Work
5A4A	Painting & Decorating
5A4B	Plastering
5A4C	Floorlaying
5A4D	Roofing Contractors
5A4E	Glass & Glazing Work
5A4F	Special Trade Contractors

6000 DISTRIBUTION HOTELS & CATERING: REPAIRS

6100	Wholesale Distribution: Except Dealing in Scrap & Waste Materials
6110	Wholesale Distribution of Agricultural Raw Materials, Live Animals, Textile Raw Materials & Semi-Manufacturers
6120	Wholesale Distribution of Fuels, Ores, Metals & Industrial Materials
6130	Wholesale Distribution of Timbers & Building Materials
6140	Wholesale Distribution of Machinery, Industrial Equipment & Vehicles
6148	Wholesale Distribution of Motor Vehicles & Parts & Accessories
6149	Wholesale Distribution of Machinery: Dealers in Tractors, Agricultural, Plant, Machine Tools, Other Machinery for use in Factories, Garages and Offices
6150	Wholesale Distribution of Household Goods, Hardware & Ironmongery
6160	Wholesale Distribution of Textiles, Clothing, Footwear & Leather Goods
6170	Wholesale Distribution of Food, Drink & Tobacco
6180	Wholesale Distribution of Pharmaceutical Medical & Other Chemist Goods
6190	Wholesale Distribution of Other Non-Food Goods: Paper; Board; Stationery, Books, Periodicals, Newspapers, Photographic, Optical Goods, Watches & Clocks, Jewellery, Toys, Sports Goods, Cycles, Perambulators
6200	Dealing in Scrap and Waste Materials
6210	Dealing in Scrap Metals: Ferrous & Non-Ferrous Scrap Metals
6220	Dealing in Other Scrap Materials or General Dealers
6300	Commission Agents
6400	Retail Distribution
6410	Food Retailing
6420	Confectioners, Tobacconists & Newsagents; Off Licences
6430	Dispensing & Other Chemists
6450	Retail Distribution of Clothing
6460	Retail Distribution of Footwear & Leather Goods
6470	Retail Distribution of Furnishing Fabrics & Household Textiles
6480	Retail Distribution of Household Goods, Hardware & Ironmongery
6500	Retail Distribution
6510	Retail Distribution of Motor Vehicles & Parts

6520	Filling Stations: Motor Fuel & Lubricants
6530	Retail Distribution of Books, Stationery & Office Supplies
6540	Other Specialised Retail Distribution (Non-Food)
6560	Mixed Retail Businesses
6600	Hotels & Catering
6610	Restaurants, Snack Bars, Cafes & Other Eating Places
6611	Licensed & Unlicensed Eating Places: No Accommodation
6612	Take-Away Food Shops
6620	Public Houses & Bars
6630	Night Clubs & Licensed Clubs
6640	Canteens & Messes
6650	Hotel Trade
6670	Other Tourist or Short-Stay Accommodation
6700	Repair of Consumer Goods & Vehicles
6710	Repair & Servicing of Motor Vehicles
6720	Repair of Footwear & Leather Goods
6730	Repair of Other Consumer Goods

7000 TRANSPORT AND COMMUNICATION

7100	Railways
7200	Other Inland Transport
7210	Urban Railways, Bus, Motor Coach & Tramway Services
7220	Other Road Passenger Transport
7230	Road Haulage
7260	Transport not Elsewhere Specified: Pipe Line Transport, Inland Water Transport, Other Transport of Land
7400	Sea Transport: Deep Sea Routes, Short Sea Routes, Domestic & Coastal Routes, Shore Bases
7500	Air Transport
7600	Supporting Services to Transport
7610	Supporting Services to Inland Transport: Land Transport, Inland Water Transport
7630	Supporting Services to Sea Transport
7640	Supporting Services to Air Transport
7700	Misc. Transport Services: Travel Agents, Freight Brokers, Storage & Warehousing
7900	Postal Services & Telecommunications
79A1	Postal Services
79A2	Telecommunications

8000 BANKING, FINANCE, INSURANCE, BUSINESS SERVICES & LEASING

8100	Banking & Finance
8140	Banking & Bill-Discounting: Central Banking Authorities, Banks & Discount Houses, Saving Banks
8150	Other Financial Institutions: Granting of Credit, Investment in Securities
8200	Insurance, Except for Compulsory Social Security
8300	Business Services
8310	Activities Auxiliary to Banking and Finance
8320	Activities Auxiliary to Insurance
8340	House and Estate Agents
8350	Legal Services

8360	Accountants, Auditors, Tax Experts
8370	Professional & Technical Services not Elsewhere Specified; Architects, Surveyors and Consulting Engineers, Technical Services
8380	Advertising
8390	Business Services
8394	Computer Services
8395	Business Services, not Elsewhere Specified
839A	Management Consultants
839B	Market Research & Public Relations Consultants
839C	Document Copying, Duplicating & Tabulating
839C	Misc. Business Services
8396	Central Offices not Allocable Elsewhere
8400	Renting of Movables
8410	Hiring out Agricultural & Horticultural Equipment
8420	Hiring out Construction Machinery & Equipment
8430	Hiring out Office Machinery & Furniture
8460	Hiring out Consumer Goods: Television & Radio Hire, Consumer Goods e.g. Photographic Equipment, Musical Instruments, Crockery
8480	Hiring out Transport Equipment
8490	Hiring out Other Movables
8500	Owning & Dealing in Real Estate

9000 OTHER SERVICES

9140	Fire Services
9150	National Defence
9190	Social Security
9200	Sanitary Services
9210	Refuse Disposal, Sanitation & Similar Services
9211	Refuse Disposal, Street Cleaning, Fumigation etc.
9212	Sewage Disposal
9230	Cleaning Services
9600	Other Services Provided to the General Public
9630	Trade Unions, Business & Professional Associations
9700	Recreational Services and Other Cultural Services
9710	Film Production, Distribution & Exhibition
9740	Radio & Television Services, Theatres, etc
9790	Sport and Other Recreational Services
9800	Personal Services

5 The product audit

What is a product?

A product (or service) is a problem-solver, in the sense that it provides what the customer needs or wants. A product consists of:

1 A core (functional performance).
2 A surround (a bundle of features and benefits).

Usually the core product has 20 per cent of the impact, yet leads to 80 per cent of the cost. The surround is the reverse of this.

Try Exercise 5.1

The product life cycle

All products or services have a life cycle which follows this pattern:

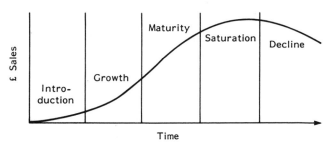

The phases of the life cycle are:

A Introduction.
B Growth.
C Maturity.
D Saturation.
E Decline.

The total life cycle depends on the type of product or service, e.g. fashion products have short life cycles.

There is a trend for life cycles of most products to get shorter as changes in technology and customer expectations make greater impact.

Each phase of the life cycle calls for different management responses.

Try Exercise 5.2

| *Diffusion of innovation* |

Some people/companies are always prepared to buy new products, while others wait until things are tried and tested. All products and services have customers which fall into these categories.

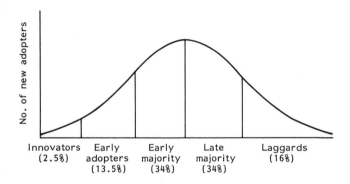

A   Innovators (2.5 per cent of total).
B   Early adopters (13.5 per cent of total).
C   Early majority (34 per cent of total).
D   Late majority (34 per cent of total).
E   Laggards (16 per cent of total).

Discovering a typology for innovators and early adopters can help in the promotion of new products.

| *Product portfolio* |

Ideally, a company should have a portfolio of products whose life cycles overlap. This guarantees continuity of income and growth potential.

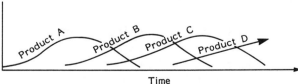

Boston Matrix

The productk portfolio can be analysed in terms of revenue-producing potential, using this technique.

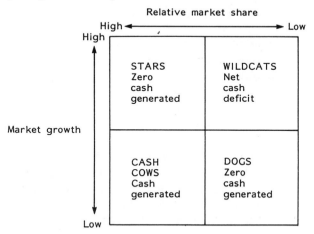

Cash cows need to generate sufficient funds to sustain stars and wildcats, and make a profit.

Try Exercise 5.3

Directional Policy Matrix

Not all companies possess the data required by the Boston Matrix (above). Similar results can be obtained using this technique. The axes become:

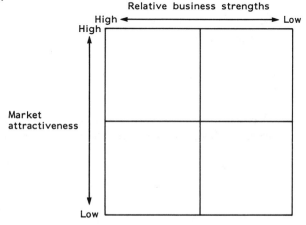

Try Exercises 5.4 and 5.5

Questions raised for the company
---

1   How useful is a brand name?

Well-known brands have successfully differentiated themselves from competing products by conveying something extra. Such differentiation enables them to command a higher price than unbranded, 'commodity' products.

2   How does market share relate to cash generation, as in the Boston matrix?

The higher the market share, the higher the output, and the lower the unit costs through economies of scale and the learning curve. Thus a company can command higher margins and generate more revenue.

3   Should 'dogs' always be killed off?

It is a question of timing. It is possible sometimes to squeeze extra earnings from a 'dog'. Sometimes a 'dog' is supportive of another product. Sometimes a 'dog' product can be profitable because it shares in the economies of scale of another product in the range.

Introduction

The exercises in this chapter are designed to help you to look at your product or service range in three different ways:

1 As a 'package' of benefits (Exercise 5.1).
2 From the point of view of their life cycles (Exercise 5.2).
3 As a total portfolio to be developed and managed in the best possible way. There are two approaches to this idea of a portfolio:

   (a) One uses the approach developed by the Boston Consulting Group, the Boston Matrix (Exercise 5.3).
   (b) The other uses the approach developed by General Electric and McKinsey, the Directional Policy Matrix (Exercise 5.4).

The final exercise in this section invites you to construct and interpret a Directional Policy Matrix for your own company (Exercise 5.5).

Exercise 5.1 Benefit package analysis

It has been shown that customers buy products and services for many reasons. Different people look for different types of benefits from the product to satisfy their needs. Here are some typical sources of customer benefits:

1   Good comparative price.
2   Well-known product/service.
3   Good after-sales service.
4   Reputable company image.
5   Low after-sales costs.
6   Prompt delivery.
7   Efficient performance.
8   Well-designed product.
9   Fashionable.
10 Ease of purchase.
11 Good quality.
12 Reliability.
13 Safety factors.

Obviously, the better one's products/services provide benefits to customers and match their needs, the more competitive they are going to be in the marketplace. The following process is designed to help you complete a benefit analysis on your products or services.

By doing this you will discover or confirm which items of your range are the strongest on the market when compared to your competitors. It should also provide you with insights about where attention might be paid to your products or services, either to improve existing customer benefits or to put emphasis on new ones.

Proceed as follows:

1   Study the customer benefits list above. Are these typical of the reasons that people buy your products or services? If you can think of others that are more pertinent to your particular business, write them down in the spaces provided.
2   Taking into account the market segments with which you do business, look at the customer benefits list and decide which are

the three most important benefits demanded by your most important segment(s). Make a note of these.

3 Now identify the next three most important benefits demanded by these customers, and also make a note of these.

4 Finally, tick any other benefits on the list that are relevant to these customers.

5 Repeat this exercise for other important segments.

6 You are now asked to transpose this information on to Worksheet 1 (an example of a completed sheet is provided in Worksheet 2). Proceed as follows:

Step 1 In column 1 list the products or services you supply. No particular order is required.

Step 2 Take the three most important benefits that you selected above and use them as headings for columns 2, 3 and 4 on the work sheet, so that column 2 represents one benefit, column 3 another and column 4 the third.

Step 3 Fill in columns 2, 3 and 4 as follows. Starting with column 2, look at the benefit heading and work down your list of products or services scoring each one on a *1 to 10 point scale*: 1 will show that the product barely supplies this particular benefit to the customer and compares badly with competitors performance, whereas a 10 score would demonstrate very high meeting of customer needs, superior to that provided by competitors. For example, if the benefit heading was 'Delivery' and, working down the list of products, the first product had a good delivery record, as good as any in the trade, then it could be allocated 9 or 10 points. If the next product on the list had a very patchy record on meeting delivery, and we knew several competitors were better, then we might only allocate 4 or 5 points, and so on. Follow the same procedure for columns 3 and 4. Note that the 1–10 scoring scale is only used on columns 2, 3 and 4 because these represent the major benefits to your customers and thus need to be weighted accordingly.

Step 4 Now take the second three most important benefits and use these as headings for columns 5, 6 and 7.

Step 5 As before rate each of your products or services against each heading, in comparison with competitor performance, but this time only *use a scoring scale of 1–6*, where again 1 point represents low provision of the benefit and 6 high. The 1–6 scoring scale is in recognition of the reduced importance these benefits have for customers.

Step 6   Finally take any other benefits you ticked above and use these as headings for column 8 and onwards as far as required.

Step 7   Again work through your list of products or services comparing them against how well they meet the benefit heading of each column, but this time only *use a 1–3 points scoring scale*. The reduced scale reflects the reduced level of importance of the customer benefits in this last group.

Step 8   Aggregate the scores you have allocated to each product or service and enter the result in the Total column.

Step 9   The product or service with the highest points score is clearly that which provides most benefits to your customers and competes favourably with the competition. Therefore allocate this product with the ranking of 1 in the Ranking column. Find the next highest total score and mark that 2 and so on. You might find some total scores so close to each other that it would be helpful to rank your products or services by groups of similar scores, rather than individually, e.g. have a first 'division', second 'division', etc., of product groupings.

Step 10   On either Worksheet 1 or a separate sheet of paper, make notes about any relevant points. For example, should some scores be qualified because of recent design improvements, are some products under threat from new competition, does the ranking reflect particular strengths or weaknesses, are there any surprises?

What are the main lessons to be learned from this type of benefit analysis for your company's products/services? What steps can you recommend to improve future product development? Use the space on p. 96 to record your thoughts.

Note. This analysis shows that 'containers' provide the best 'benefits package' when compared to the rest of the product range. In contrast, 'water butts' provide least benefits, falling down on price, delivery and design. This analysis enables a company to see where it needs to work at the 'product surround' to become more effective.

WORKSHEET 1 Benefit package analysis (Ex. 5.1)

	MAJOR BENEFITS			MEDIUM BENEFITS			LESSER BENEFITS													
	Low score 1		High 10	Low score 1		High 6	Low score 1						High score 3					Total	Ranking	Notes, Observations, Qualifying comments, Strengths, etc.
Col. nos. (1)	(2)	(3)	(4)	(5)	(6)	(7)	8	9	10	11	12	13	14	15	16	17	18			
Customer benefits / Prods or services																				

WORKSHEET 2 Benefit package analysis (Ex. 5.1) – a Plastics Processing Company

	MAJOR BENEFITS			MEDIUM BENEFITS			LESSER BENEFITS													
	Low score 1		High 10	Low score 1		High 6	Low score 1						High score 3					Total	Ranking	Notes, Observations, Qualifying comments, Strengths, etc.
Col. nos. (1)	(2)	(3)	(4)	(5)	(6)	(7)	8	9	10	11	12	13	14	15	16	17	18			
Customer benefits / Prods or services	Price	Quality	Delivery	Design	Safety	Reliability	Our image	After-sales service	Packaging	Comprehensive range								Total	Ranking	
Water butts	5	8	5	3	6	6	1	1	2	2								39	4	Check costing and deliveries
Containers	8	8	7	5	6	3	3	2	3	2								47	1	Again business difficult to improve except on delivery and reliability
Toy (compts)	3	8	9	5	6	5	1	1	2	2								42	2	Doesn't always mix with other work
Cones for road works, etc.	7	8	6	4	6	5	1	1	3	1								42	2	Work at price and delivery. Also need to improve designs and range

Personal notes

Exercise 5.2 Life-cycle analysis

It is universally accepted that all products or services go through a life cycle of five stages – introduction, growth, maturity, saturation and, ultimately, decline.

Depending upon the nature of the particular product and its market, the life cycle can be of short or long duration. Similarly, different products will have different levels of sales. Nevertheless, allowing for these differences in 'width' and 'height', product life-cycle curves all have a remarkably similar and consistent shape. It is because of consistency of the life cycle curve that this aspect of the product audit becomes such a powerful analytical tool.

The following exercise is designed to help you construct a life-cycle analysis for your company's products or services. By doing this it will help to focus on information that will be used in setting marketing objectives and strategies.

1 Using Worksheet 1, invent a suitable scale for the sales volume axis, i.e. one that will encompass the sales peaks you have had or are likely to experience in your business.

2 At the position marked Current sales, record the levels of sales volume for your products or services. You will have to select the time-scale you use. If your products are short-lived, perhaps you might have to calculate sales figures in terms of days or weeks. For longer-lived products, perhaps annual sales figures will be more appropriate.

3 Taking each product in turn, plot a life-cycle curve based upon the historical data at your disposal, e.g. if in 2 above you decided that a monthly sales analysis would be necessary to capture the movement on the life-cycle curves, then check back through your sales records and plot the sales volume for each product at monthly intervals.

4 From the life-cycle curves you have drawn, extend those into the future where extrapolation looks feasible, i.e. where a distinct pattern exists. You should finish up with a worksheet looking something like Worksheet 2.

5 Make notes about your key findings from this exercise in the space below.

6 So far you have only looked at your products in isolation. Now on

a separate piece of paper (or on the same worksheet if it doesn't cause too much confusion), compare each life-cycle pattern of your major products or services with the *total market* life cycle for each one. Do your product patterns mirror the market life cycle? Are your sales falling, while the total market sales are steady or increasing? Is the reverse happening? Many outcomes will be possible, but whatever they are, you are asked to explain them and to write in the space below what these comparisons between the total market and your sales tell you about your product/service range and its future prospects. If you find it difficult to establish total market life cycles then refer to the 'Guide to market maturity' on p. 100.

7   Finally, and to demonstrate that this examination of product life cycles is not just an intellectual exercise, prepare a short presentation for one of your senior colleagues, or, better still, your boss, following the instructions given on the 'Special project brief' on p. 99.

Notes

WORKSHEET 1   Life-cycle analysis (Ex. 5.2)

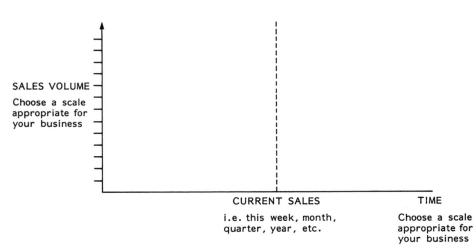

SALES VOLUME

Choose a scale appropriate for your business

CURRENT SALES
i.e. this week, month, quarter, year, etc.

TIME
Choose a scale appropriate for your business

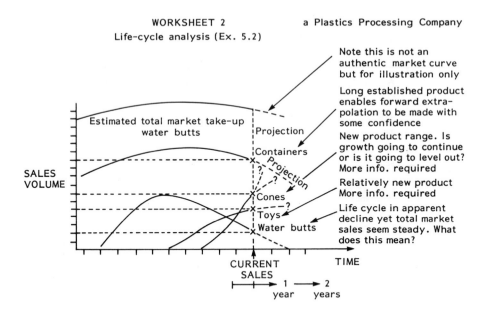

WORKSHEET 2
Life-cycle analysis (Ex. 5.2)

a Plastics Processing Company

GUIDE TO MARKET MATURITY

The following checklist is used by one major company to help it determine where its markets are on the life cycle.

SPECIAL PROJECT BRIEF

Product life cycles

Take any product you know well and prepare a short presentation (say 10 minutes) which covers the following areas/questions:

1 Brief product description – your definition of the market it serves.
2 Your estimates of the product's current point in the life-cycle curve.
3 Your reasons for believing it is at this point.
4 Your estimate of the length and shape of this life cycle.
5 Your reasons for this estimate.
6 Your predictions of the prospects for this product over the next 3 years.
7 Your reasons for these predictions.

GUIDE TO MARKET MATURITY

The following checklist is used by one major company to help it determine where its markets are on the life cycle.

Maturity stage / Factor	Embryonic	Growth	Mature saturation	Declining
1 Growth rate	Normally much greater than GNP (on small base)	Sustained growth above GNP. New customers. New suppliers. Rate decelerates towards end of stage	Approximately equals GNP	Declining demand. Market shrinks as users' needs change
2 Predictability of growth potential	Hard to define accurately. Small portion of demand being satisfied. Market forecasts differ widely	Greater percentage of demand is met and upper limits of demand becoming clearer. Discontinuities such as price reductions based on economies of scale may occur	Potential well defined. Competition specialized to satisfy needs of specific segments	Known and limited
3 Product line proliferation	Specialized lines to meet needs of early customers	Rapid expansion	Proliferation slows or ceases	Lines narrow as unprofitable products dropped
4 Number of competitors	Unpredictable	Reaches maximum. New entrants attracted by growth and high margins. Some consolidation begins toward end of stage	Entrenched positions established. Further shakeout of marginal competitors	New entrants unlikely. Competitors continue to decline
5 Market share	Unstable. Shares react unpredictably to entrepreneurial insights and timing	Increasing stability. Typically, a few competitors emerging as strong	Stable, with a few companies often controlling much of the industry	Highly concentrated, sometimes fragmented if market becomes segmented
6 Customer stability	Trial usage with little customer loyalty	Some loyalty. Repeat usage with many seeking alternative suppliers	Well developed buying patterns, with customer loyalty. Competitors understand purchase dynamics and it is difficult for a new supplier to win over accounts	Extremely stable. Suppliers dwindle and customers less motivated to seek alternatives
7 Ease of entry	Normally easy. No one dominates. Customers' expectations uncertain. If barriers exist they are usually technology, capital or fear of the unknown	More difficult. Market franchises and/or economies of scale may exist, yet new business is still available without directly confronting competition	Difficult. Market leaders established. New business must be 'won' from others	Little or no incentive to enter
8 Technology	Plays an important role in matching product characteristics to market needs. Frequent product changes	Product technology vital early, while process technology more important later in this stage	Process and material substitution focus. Product requirements well known and relatively undemanding. May be a thrust to renew the industry via new technology	Technological content is known, stable and accessible

Exercise 5.3   Case study: International Bearings Ltd (IBL)

The objectives of this case study are as follows:

1 To demonstrate a useful method of reviewing, at any point in time, the commercial implications of decision-making for a company with a number of different products, in different markets, at different stages of growth, maturity or decline. This is known as a product portfolio. This method was introduced by the Boston Consulting Group and is known as the Boston Matrix.
2 To demonstrate the application of the Boston Matrix by using a case study in which an industrial company competes with a number of competitors in a number of different market segments.
3 To give the user practical experience by working through the situation analysis and decision-making process illustrated in the case study.
4 To encourage the user to apply the principles learned in the case study to his/her own commercial situation.

You are asked to write down your answers to the questions on the worksheet provided. The correct answers are given in Appendix 1. Further details on the principles of the Boston Matrix are given in Appendix 2. Details of the information-gathering techniques to help users to construct their own Boston Matrix are provided in Appendix 3.

International Bearings Limited (IBL) sells a number of fast moving industrial products in a market with about sixty competitors, most of whom are relatively small. Eight companies, including IBL, are significant in terms of size. IBL has seven major product groups.

The situation of IBL is shown in Table 5.1.

DEFINITIONS OF HEADINGS IN TABLE 5.1

Relative market share is the ratio of your market share to the share of the largest competitor in your market. Thus, if you have 10 per cent market share and your biggest competitor has 40 per cent market share, then the ratio (or relative market share) is 1:4. This is usually expressed as 0.25:1. If you have a market share of 20 per cent and your biggest

Table 5.1

Product	Sales volume (units)	Relative market share	Current market growth (year 1, %)	Forecast market growth (year 3, %)
1	1,500	*	20	25
2	1,300	2:1	9	6
3	1,000	0.9:1	12	25
4	1,000	0.6:1	10	2
5	900	0.5:1	5	3
6	800	0.2:1	3	0
7	500	0.1:1	22	25
Total	7,000			

* This ratio has been omitted, as it forms part of the exercise later in this case study.

competitor has a market share of 10 per cent, then the ratio would be 2:1.

Current market growth is the percentage growth in sales of a product in a market over the previous year's sales. Thus, if a market was 100 last year and 120 this year, then the growth would be 20 per cent.

Forecast market growth is the annual rate at which you believe the market will grow in the future. For example, you may forecast that the market will grow by 10 per cent in Year 2 and 20 per cent in Year 3. So 10 per cent forecast market growth for Year 2 is Year 1 figure of 120 × 10 per cent: answer: 132. For Year 3 it is Year 2 figure of 132 × 20: answer: 158.4.

The situation of the IBL product 1's absolute market share, compared to the remainder of the market, is shown in Table 5.2.

Table 5.2

	IBL	B	C	D	E	F	G	H	Others (about 50)
					Companies				
Absolute market share (%)	15	10	8	8	8	7	5	5	34

IBL has 15 per cent absolute market share. Table 5.1 states that figure represents 1,500, so:

$$\frac{1500}{1} \times \frac{100}{15} = 10,000$$

Which is the current year total market size for product 1.

DEFINITIONS OF HEADINGS IN TABLE 5.2

Absolute market share is the percentage of a total market that your product enjoys. For example, total market size = 100 units per annum. Your sales are 25 per annum. Therefore you have 25 per cent absolute market share. Absolute market share is expressed as a percentage of the total market.

As defined above, relative market share is expressed as a ratio, e.g. 2:1. This compares your market share and degree of dominance to one other competitor.

The market forecast for IBL's product 1 is as shown in Table 5.3.

Table 5.3

	Current year (%)	Year 2 (%)	Year 3 (%)
Actual production	20		
Forecast growth		22	25

IBL's own forecast for product 1 is shown in Table 5.4:

Table 5.4

	Current year	Year 2	Year 3
Actual sales	1,500 units		
Sales forecast		1,650 units	1,815 units

Please note that the forecast market growth for product 1 in Table 5.3 is different from IBL's own forecast of product 1 in Table 5.4.

A senior executive from company B has recently joined IBL, as a result of which IBL has received some accurate market intelligence about company B's product 1, which competes with IBL's own product 1. This is shown in Table 5.5.

Table 5.5

	Current year	Year 2	Year 3
Actual sales	1,000 units		
Sales forecast		1,500 units	1,562 units

Please answer the following questions:

Question 1
What is IBL's relative market share for product 1? Remember that relative market share is a ratio, e.g. 3.5:1.

  Write your answer to this question and all others on the answer sheet provided in Appendix 1, p. 109
Question 2
What will IBL's relative market share be for product 1 in year 3? Limit your answer to two decimal places.

  For this question you may need to refer to Tables 5.4 and 5.5.
Question 3
What is the annual growth of the market for product 1?
Question 4
What will be the total market volume for product 1 in year 3?
Question 5
What is the absolute market share of IBL's product 1 in year 3?

  Round up your answer to the nearest whole number.
Question 6
Is the market growth in the current year, high or low, relative to the industry average of 10%?
Question 7
Relative market share and market growth are important factors a company should consider when appraising its product portfolio. Rather than looking at masses of figures, which are hard to interpret individually, the Boston Consulting Group (BCG), devised a matrix to show these two factors as a graphic drawing.

  The Matrix is square and the relative market share (RMS) is placed on the horizontal axis. The imaginary lines are vertical. Market growth is measured on the vertical axis. See Figure 5.1.

  The lowest figure (usually zero) is at the bottom, and, depending on

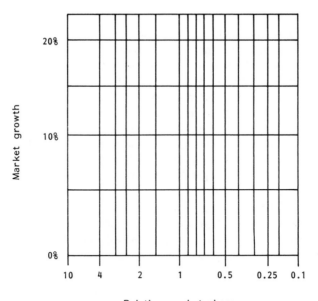

Figure 5.1   *Boston Matrix*

the industry, up to 20 per cent. (This upper figure may vary, e.g. an established product may be under 10 per cent or a new product may be in excess of 100 per cent).

The decision on what constitutes 'high' or 'low' growth is thus dependent on the industry. The decision is yours. In this case we have chosen to use 10 per cent as the dividing line between high growth, i.e. greater than 10 per cent, or low growth, i.e. less than 10 per cent.

In the example we are using a scale ending at approximately 20 per cent. The imaginary lines run horizontally across the matrix.

Take the products numbered 1 to 7 and, using Table 5.1 data, place them at the correct coordinates for relative market share and market growth. For this purpose, a matrix is provided on the answer sheet on p. 109

Question 8

The next stage is to make these coordinates into circles. This is necessary so that the executive completing the matrix can understand the relative importance to the company of the products which appear in the matrix. Some circles will be bigger than others, indicating a greater contribution to turnover.

It is also important because the executive can forecast the size of each circle and its likely position on the matrix in, say, 3 years' time. He could, for example, show the position and size of the circles if the company continued with its current policies, or he could show where they will be if different policies are pursued.

In this case the diameter of each circle represents the relative contribution of each product to the total volume of IBL. The scale adopted is your decision. It generally depends on the size of paper you are using. For example, you may choose 1 mm = 10,000 units, so a product selling 50,000 units will measure 5mm and so on for each product. (To be technically correct, we should take the square root of each of the sales volumes to determine the proportionate area of each circle. However, for the sake of simplicity, we have used the method described above.)

On Figure 5.1 the next task is to convert the coordinates marked 1–7 into circles representing the relative contribution of each product. First, however, using a scale of 1mm = 100 units of sales volume, calculate the correct diameter for each of the seven products and write your answers in the answer sheet provided in Appendix 1. Next, draw circles on the matrix provided, using the answers given above for the diameters.

A short explanation of the principles behind the Boston Matrix is given in Appendix 2, p.111. Understanding the Matrix will enable you to answer the questions which follow.

Question 9
Do you think IBL currently have a well-balanced product portfolio? Give reasons for your answer.

Question 10
State the forecast position of IBL's Product 1 in Year 3.

Write in figures the RMS (including a decimal point and colon, e.g. 5.2:1). Write in figures the MG (e.g. 50%).

Question 11
Using a scale of 1mm = 100 units of sales volume, what will the diameter of the circle for IBL's product 1 be in year 3?

State your answer in figures to the nearest whole number.

Question 12
Are the signs ahead good, comparing the forecast position of IBL's product 1 with the current situation? Give reasons for your answer.

Question 13
What is happening to IBL's main product in the current situation? Choose from the options A-D listed below:

A Losing market share in a declining market.
B Gaining market share in a growing market.
C Losing market share in a growing market.
D Losing profitability in a stable market.

Question 14

What policy should IBL pursue for product 1? Choose from the options listed below:

A   Increase price, reduce promotion.
B   Reduce price, reduce promotion.
C   Hold price, reduce promotion.
D   Hold price, increase promotion.
E   Reduce price, increase promotion.
F   Increase price, increase promotion.

Question 15
In this situation it was decided to maintain product 1's market share by investing in it, to grow at the same rate of forecast market growth of 20, 22, 25 per cent. Which other products from the list below would you invest in? Choose from the combinations A, B, C, or D below:

A   Products 2 and 5.
B   Products 3 and 7.
C   Products 3 and 6.
D   Products 4 and 7.

Question 16
Select one product's position you should maintain from the options of products 2 to 7 below?
   Select product 2, 3, 4, 5, 6 or 7.
Question 17
Which combinations of products might it be appropriate to manage for cash from the options below?

A   Products 5, 6 and 7.
B   Products 3, 4 and 5.
C   Products 4, 5 and 6.
D   Products 4, 5 and 7.

Having completed this case study, you should by now fully understand the principles and the methodology of the Boston Matrix.
   There are, of course other approaches to portfolio management. However, before considering these, using the methodology explained in this case study, produce a Boston Matrix for your own company's products.
   Some practical suggestions for producing your own Boston Matrix, now follow:

1   Try not to use more than ten products. If in doubt, choose the 20

per cent of your products that account for the majority of your turnover.

2 If this still proves to be too many, then find some way of grouping your products until you have a manageable number.

3 Directors and senior managers doing this additional exercise may prefer to use companies, divisions, countries, markets, or strategic business units instead of products. They all work just as well.

4 Great care is needed in defining 'market' share. Remember, a 'market' consists of all other brands that satisfy the same needs as your brand.

5 Forecast the size and position of your products in say, 3 years' time. Ask yourself:

   (*a*) Is it a well-balanced portfolio?
   (*b*) Are you pursuing appropriate policies for each of your products or business areas?

WORKSHEET FOR ANSWERS   CASE STUDY IBL

See page 109

APPENDIX 1   CORRECT ANSWERS TO THE IBL CASE STUDY C EX.5.3)

1   1.5:1 (1500 ÷ 1000)
2   1.16:1 (1815 ÷ 1562)
3   20% 22% 25% (from Table 5.3)
4   Table 5.1 gave product 1 sales as 1,500. Table 5.2 gave absolute market share of 15% for IBL. Market size in year

$$1 = \frac{1,500}{1} \times \frac{100}{15} = 10,000.$$

Thus, market size for year 3 is found from the % figures in Table 5.3. Thus, $10,000 \times 22\% \times 25\% = 15,250$

5   12% from Table 5.3, year 3 (1815), divide that by the answer to question 4 (15,250) = 11.9
6   High. In each of the three years the market is forecast to grow at a higher rate than 10% (20%, 22%, 25%)

7	RMS	RMG
1	1.5:1	20%
2	2:1	9%
3	0.9:1	12%
4	0.6:1	10%
5	0.5:1	5%

Case study IBL

Last name

First name

Question number	Answer
1	
2	
3	
4	Yr 1.... Yr 2.... Yr 3....
5	
6	
7	

Product	RMS	RMG
1		
2		
3		
4		
5		
6		
7		

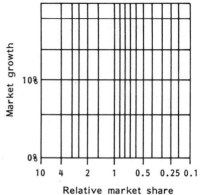

8	1
	2
	3
	4
	5
	6
	7
9	

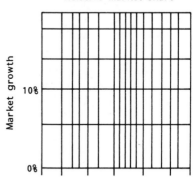

10	
11	
12	
13	
14	
15	
16	
17	

6 0.2:1   3%
7 0.1:1   22%

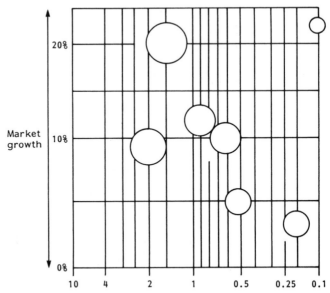

Figure 5.2 *Coordinates for RMS and RMG*

8 1 15mm
   2 13mm
   3 10mm
   4 10mm
   5 9mm
   6 8mm
   7 5mm
9 Yes. There is one significant cash cow. 'Cash cow' product 1 is market leader in a fast-growing market (a 'star'). Product 3 is almost market leader in a fast-growing market. Product 7 is a 'question mark'. Products 4, 5 and 6 are 'dogs', but this is not a problem as long as products 2, 3 and 7 are managed appropriately.
10 1.16:1 25%
11 1815 18
12 No. IBL's main product is losing market share in a growing market.
13 C is the best answer, but not the only one. You may wish to consider other factors, including company policy, e.g. improving the product.
14 D
15 B
16 2
17 C

APPENDIX 2   THE PRINCIPLES OF THE BOSTON MATRIX (EX.5.3)

The principles of the Boston Matrix can be applied to practical commercial situations for improving business planning and assisting decision-taking where a company has a number of products.

What is the Boston Matrix?

The Boston Matrix is used for what is known as product portfolio planning. It uses graphic models to develop a relationship between two or more variables known to be of significance in the corporate context.

The two main variables are relative market share and market growth. Both have been shown to be strongly related to profitability. In general, the bigger a firm's relative market share is, the lower its costs are, and the bigger its return on investment. The rate of market growth also has a significant impact on a company's performance.

The Boston Consulting Group combined these two variables in the form of a simple matrix, which has been shown to have profound implications for the firm, especially in respect of cashflow. '

The Boston Matrix classifies a firm's products according to their cash usage and their cash generation along the two dimensions, relative market share and market growth.

Why use a matrix rather than a sheet of figures?

The Boston Matrix shows graphically the positions in terms of relative market share and market growth of a number of products at a glance. Presented in a matrix, it is easier for an executive to see the relationship between a number of different products. It is also a very powerful presentation device for planning purposes.

How is the Boston Matrix used?

Different products have to be managed in ways appropriate to their different business environments and according to their different strengths and weaknesses. There is a need to maintain strong and profitable products. There is a need to invest in new products as existing products muture and die.

The Boston Matrix provides a powerful vehicle for assessing a firm's position as represented by its portfolio or products. Finally, it enables appropriate policies to be developed for each product to ensure continuing growth in sales and profits.

Some examples of the use of the Boston Matrix.

The Boston Consulting Group chose picturesque labels to attach to each of the four categories of products to give some indication of the prospects for products in each quadrant. Pages 96 to 100 in the textbook *Marketing Plans: how to prepare them; how to use them* (Butterworth-Heinemann, 1989) give full details of the four categories:

- Star.
- Cash cow.
- Question mark.
- Dog.

'Cash cows' are leaders in markets where there is little additional growth. They are excellent generators of cash and tend to use little. 'Stars' are leaders in high growth markets. They tend to generate a lot of cash, but also use a lot because of growth market conditions. 'Question marks' have not yet achieved a dominant market position, and so do not generate much cash. They can, however, use a lot of cash because of growth market conditions. Sometimes these are referred to as 'wildcats'. 'Dogs' have little future and are often a cash drain on the company.

The art of portfolio management now becomes clearer. We should be seeking to use surplus cash generated by 'cash cows' to invest in 'stars' and a selected number of 'question marks'.

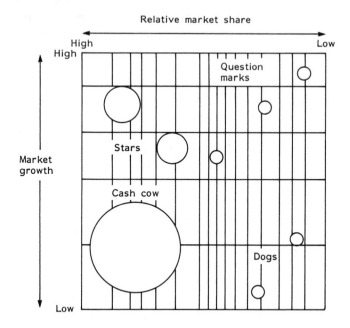

Figure 5.3   *Well-balanced product portfolio*

Figure 5.3 shows a well-balanced product portfolio. There is one large 'cash cow', two sizeable 'stars', and three emerging products in high growth markets. There are only two small 'dogs'.

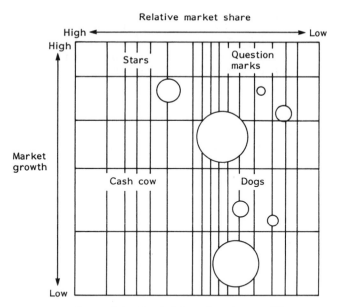

Figure 5.4   *Poorly balanced product portfolio*

Figure 5.4 shows a poorly balanced product portfolio. The company has no 'cash cows'. There is only one small 'star'. It has three 'question marks' and three 'dogs', one of which is a sizeable product. This company probably has cashflow problems.

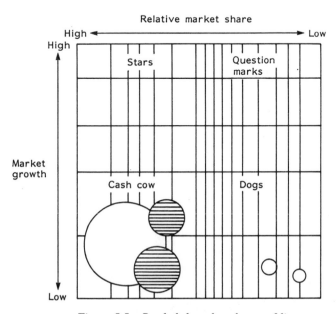

Figure 5.5   *Poorly balanced product portfolio*

Figure 5.5 also shows a poorly balanced product portfolio. This company is probably cash-rich, with three sizeable 'cash cows'. However, all the danger signs are evident. There are no new products coming along to replace the 'cash cows', which may well decline in the future.

Exercise 5.4 International Bearings Ltd – directional policy case study

The main business of IBL is the sale of a portfolio of bearings and assemblies based on bearings to a variety of end-use markets in Europe, in which IBL is a very significant and well-established player. IBL manufactures products in five different locations, each making only part of the product range to achieve maximum production cost benefits.

Each country has its own sales organization marketing the whole range. These national organizations have two salesforces, one dealing with original equipment manufacturers (OEMs), the other selling via independent distributors to the replacement market, except for large customers, who are handled direct.

There is a European marketing organization responsible for strategy in terms of product range development, pricing structures, corporate promotion, etc. Under the European Marketing Director, it is split into market sector managers (e.g. automotive, electrical machinery, etc.) who develop strategies for their own segments. The European marketing organization reports to the Director-Europe, as do the country general managers, to whom the country sales organizations report.

In the mid-1980s a new European marketing director was appointed. His first task was to develop a long-term strategic marketing plan. From a detailed study of past and present performance, he noted that, though historically successful, European market share was hovering at around 28 per cent and that profits, although satisfactory, were mainly stagnant. These results were being caused by lack of growth in some key markets, e.g. automotive, and intensified competition, notably from Japan.

One of the key effects of these market and competitive pressures that he noted as he travelled around Europe was a lack of vision and motivation in the national sales organizations. During the late 1970s/early 1980s, under a policy of decentralization, they had been left largely alone to do the best they could in what were difficult recessionary times.

He concluded that performance could be significantly improved, especially as there were signs that some key segments were becoming buoyant, and he obtained top management approval to develop a long-term plan, 'Going for growth'. The key objective agreed by the board was 'To increase European market share to 35 per cent by the end of the planning period in 3 years'.

In order to achieve this, the European marketing director knew that he would have to look at the product/market portfolio in a different way and to establish realistic strategies in the areas most likely to produce dividends. To help him do this, he decided to construct a directional policy matrix.

As you work through this case study you will observe how the task was tackled. You will appreciate the calculations and the reasons behind decision-making.

The marketing director first set his market research manager the task of selecting SIC (Standard Industrial Classification) categories, based on his current bearing business in order to select those segments best suited for investment. (The governments of most countries keep records of industrial activity under SIC listings. The SIC listings in most countries of the world are comparable for the purpose of comparisons and cross-references.)

His market research manager came up with the information in Table 5.6.

Table 5.6

SIC category	Market size (£ million)	Growth (%)	Competitive intensity	Profitability (%)	Vulnerability
1 Meat-processing	20	12	Low	17	Low
2 Automotive	200	2	High	<10	High
3 Local govt	20	4	High	<10	High
4 Food-processing	40	10	Medium	16	Medium
5 Forestry	20	11	Low	20	Medium
6 Electrical	100	0	High	<10	High
7 Agricultural	40	2	Medium	<10	High
8 Chemical	15	15	Low	16	Low

The first stage is to apply the information in Table 5.6, and to establish positions on the vertical scale labelled 'market attractiveness' on the directional policy matrix (DPM). However, before that can be done, some criteria about what constitutes an attractive market for International Bearings have to be established and weighted in terms of their relative importance. (A list of possible attractiveness factors is given in Appendix 1, p.125.)

Precisely how this is done is a matter of management judgement, but it is important to follow three golden rules:

1 Never do this in isolation.

2 Make sure your key colleagues are in agreement over the criteria and weightings to be used.
3 Whenever quantitative information, or techniques such as market research, is available, it should be used in preference to opinions, no matter how well founded these opinions might be.

Being aware of these rules, the European marketing director got his marketing team together and they came up with the information in Table 5.7. With this new information available to him, the marketing director was able to begin calculating the market attractiveness 'scores' for different industries.

Table 5.7

Factor	Scoring criteria*			Weighting
	10–7	*6–3*	*2–1*	*(%)***
1 Market size (m)	>100	33–100	<33	15
2 Volume growth (units)	>10%	5–9%	<5%	25
3 Competitive intensity	Low	Medium	High	15
4 Profitability	>15%	10–15%	<10%	30
5 Vulnerability	Low	Medium	High	15

* The precise score given is a matter of management judgement.
** The weightings given to each factor are also a matter of management judgement.

From Table 5.6, it will be seen that the market size is £20 m. From Table 5.7 you will see that any category £<33 m is scored in the range 1–2 points, with a weighting of 15, so in this case a score of 1 can be given. It is then multiplied by the weighting of 15 per cent to give a result of 0.15. You will observe from this that you must use your judgement in deciding whether the score should be 1 or 2 (or something in between).

This inevitably means that there will be a range of possible answers. In this case the range could be 0.15 to 0.3.

Bearing this in mind, see if you can complete the market attractiveness scoring for meat-processing in Table 5.8. You can check if your answer is correct by looking at Table 5.9 and comparing your result with that produced by the company.

You will note that the remaining criteria of attractiveness were all high, and because of that, each carried a score of between 7 and 10. Depending on the actual scores given, the total, after being multiplied by the weighting factor, could fall within the range given in Table 5.9, shown in brackets.

Table 5.8 **Meat-processing**

	Scoring criteria		Weighting (%)		Total
Market size	1	X	15		= 0.15
Growth	–	X	25		= _____
Competitive intensity	–	X	15		= _____
Profitability	–	X	30		= _____
Vulnerability	–	X	15		= _____
				Total	
					_____

Table 5.9 *Meat-processing*

	Scoring criteria		Weighting (%)	Total	
Market size	1	X	15	=0.15	
Growth	– (7–10)	X	25	=_____	(1.75–2.5)
Competitive intensity	– (7–10)	X	15	=_____	(2.1–3.0)
Profitability	– (7–10)	X	30	=_____	(1.05–1.5)
Vulnerability	– (7–10)	X	15	=_____	(1.05–1.5)
			Total	_____	(6.10–8.65)

It is important that you are clear about how the total market attractiveness score is calculated. If you feel that you would like another opportunity to work at this, see if you can arrive at a score for the automotive industry. All the information you require is in Tables 5.10 and 5.11.

Table 5.10 **Automotive**

	Scoring criteria		Weighting (%)		Total
Market size	–	X	15		= _____
Growth	–	X	25		= _____
Competitive intensity	–	X	15		= _____
Profitability	–	X	30		= _____
Vulnerability	–	X	15		= _____
				Total	_____

The answer to Table 5.10 is shown in Table 5.11. Again, you will note that there has to be an element of judgement in the scoring.

Table 5.11 **Automotive**

	Scoring criteria	Weighting (%)	Total
Market size	– (7–10)	X 15	= _____ (1.05–1.5)
Growth	– (1–2)	X 25	= _____ (0.25–0.5)
Competitive intensity	– (1–2)	X 15	= _____ (0.15–0.3)
Profitability	– (1–2)	X 30	= _____ (0.3–0.6)
Vulnerability	– (1–2)	X 15	= _____ (0.15–0.3)
		Total	_____ (2.35–3.2)

From these two examples you can see the idea of how the figures are arrived at for *market attractiveness*. As you will see, the final figures are within a minimum and maximum range for each category. For the purpose of this case study, the figures are stated as below:

1 Meat-processing   0.65
2 Automotive   2.35
3 Local government   1.25
4 Food-processing   7.45
5 Forestry   8.05
6 Electrical   2.35
7 Agriculture   2.4
8 Chemical   0.65

Now we will look at how the calculations are made for establishing the relative positions of these markets on the horizontal axis, or *business strengths*, of the DPM.

Two tables, similar to Tables 5.6 and 5.7, are given. The first, Table 5.12, shows factor, scoring criteria, and weighting; and the next, Table 5.13, the marketing team's assessment of the firm's competitive strengths in each of the SIC categories.

Table 5.12

Factor	Scoring criteria*			Weighting (%)**
	10–7	6–3	2–1	
1 Product advantage	High	Medium	Low	25
2 Image with market	Excellent	Average	Poor	50
3 Ability to supply engineering support	High	Medium	Low	25

*   The precise score given is a matter of management judgement.
**   The weightings given to each factor are also a matter of management judgement. Remember the three golden rules still apply:

1 Key colleagues should be in agreement.
2 Do not do this in isolation.
3 Use quantitative techniques to determine criteria whenever available.

There are, of course, a whole range of possible factors which could be viewed as business strengths. Many are listed in Appendix 2, p.127. However, from International Bearing's point of view, in order to assess the business strengths in each of the eight markets, the marketing director was only concerned with the three key factors given in Table 5.13.

Table 5.13 **Marketing team's assessment**

SIC category	Product advantage	Image	Engineering support
1 Meat-processing	High	Excellent	High
2 Automotive	Low	Excellent	High
3 Local government	Low	Poor	Medium
4 Food-processing	High	Excellent	High
5 Forestry	Low	Poor	Low
6 Electrical	Low	Poor	Low
7 Agricultural	High	Excellent	Medium
8 Chemical	Low	Poor	Medium

Table 5.13 uses the criteria to assess the firm's competitive strengths. The process to transfer the information from Tables 5.14 and 5.15 is similar to the previous exercise done with Tables 5.6 and 5.7.

Take meat-processing as an example. The product advantage is high in Table 5.13. In Table 5.12 a high assessment may be scored between 7 and 10. The weighting is 25 per cent. You may choose 9 for product advantage, so this, multiplied by the weighting of 25 per cent, gives 2.25 as the score. Table 5.14 shows how the scoring could be completed and the possible range of the end result.

Table 5.14 **Meat-processing**

	Scoring criteria	Weighting (%)	Total
Product advantage	9	X 25	= _____ 2.25
Image	– (7–10)	X 50	= _____ (3.5–5.0)
Engineering support	– (7–10)	X 25	= _____ (1.75–2.5)
		Total	_____ (7.0–10)

If you would like the practice, work out the score for automotive (Table 5.15). The answer is given in Table 5.16.

Table 5.15 **Automotive**

	Scoring criteria		Weighting (%)	Total
Product advantage	–	X	25	= _____
Image	–	X	50	= _____
Engineering support	–	X	25	= _____
			Total	_____

Table 5.16 **Automotive**

	Scoring criteria		Weighting	Total	
Product advantage	– (1–2)	X	25	= _____	(0.25–0.50)
Image	– (7–10)	X	50	= _____	(3.5–5.0)
Engineering support	– (7–10)	X	25	= _____	(1.75–8.0)
			Total	_____	(5.5–2.5)

Using this technique, the marketing director made the following assessment of the business strengths for the eight product areas:

1	Meat-processing	8.75
2	Automotive	7.75
3	Local government	2.0
4	Food-processing	10.0
5	Forestry	1.0
6	Electrical	1.0
7	Agriculture	9.0
8	Chemical	2.25

He was now in a position to start plotting the various markets on the directional policy matrix. You will note that, because of the way the scoring and weighting were established, i.e. a maximum of 10 points and the highest weighting being 100 per cent, the highest possible total is ten. Therefore the matrix can be designed with each side being of 10 units length. Equally, because of this scoring system, 5 represents a genuine mid-point, in the sense that scores above this figure are tending towards the 'more attractive' or 'higher business strengths', whereas those below 5 are, relatively speaking, the poor relations. (Please note, however, the methodological comments in Appendix 1, p.125)

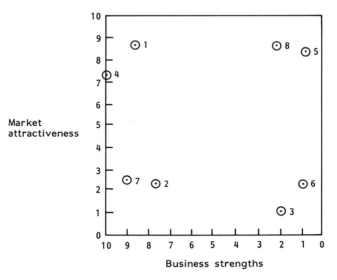

Figure 5.6

The numbers at the intersections refer to the markets as listed above. Thus 1 is meat-processing, 2 automotive and so on.

The DPM is almost complete. What remains to be done is to indicate the sales volume for each of the markets. This is achieved by drawing a circle proportional to the sales volume at each of the market location points that have just been plotted.

It is often a matter of trial and error to establish the correct basis for drawing these circles. If, for example, the largest sales volume was 1,500 and the smallest was 300, you may decide that every 100 units = 3 mm of diameter. So, 1,500 is shown as 15 units × 3 = 45 mm, and 300 as 3 units × 3 = 9 mm. If this scale is too small or large, then change it to suit the diagram.

This is the sales volume for each category:

SIC		Sales volume
1	Meat-processing	1,500
2	Automotive	1,300
3	Local government	1,000
4	Food-processing	900
5	Forestry	800
6	Electrical	700
7	Agricultural	500
8	Chemical	300

Continuing with the example of 100 units = 3 mm of diameter, we get this representative sales volume for each category:

SIC		Sales volume	Diameter
1	Meat-processing	1,500	45
2	Automotive	1,300	39
3	Local government	1,000	30
4	Food-processing	900	27
5	Forestry	800	24
6	Electrical	700	21
7	Agricultural	500	15
8	Chemical	300	9

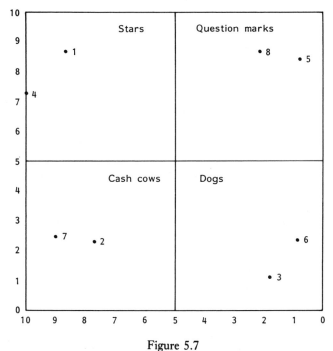

Figure 5.7

Figure 5.7 shows the circles representing the sales volume of each category in the correct locations on the matrix.

This form of presentation is superior in terms of the impact and clarity given to the data presentation shown in Tables 5.6, 5.7, 5.12, 5.13. It clearly shows at a glance:

- The relative importance of each market to the business.
- The relative attractiveness of each market.
- The company's relative strengths in each market.

The same names can be given to each quadrant as are used in the Boston Matrix, although you should note that it is not necessary to give any names at all to each of the boxes. The Boston Matrix names are used here only because you are by now familiar with them.

Faced with the above information, if you were in the marketing director's position, what would be your objectives and strategies for each of the markets?

Write your proposals on a separate piece of paper. When you have completed this task, you can check your answers with those of the marketing director below.

Here is how the marketing director of International Bearings used the DPM to arrive at objectives and strategies for each market:

1 In the event, he concentrated much effort on growing the very attractive meat-process and food processing segments, because he was well placed to do this and because he was able to add value in so doing. In the next 3 years, he added a further 2,000 units of very profitable volume to these two segments.

2 Automotive and agriculture were maintained by aggressive pricing whenever he had to in order to keep the business, but he cut down dramatically on costs. In these businesses he succeeded in increasing volume sales from 1,000 to 2,000 units during the next 3 years. Margins were down, but so were costs.

3 He invested some resources to improve his position in the chemical segment, paying for it by taking money out of the forestry segment. Here he grew his volume from 300 to 700 units.

4 Finally, he did not invest in either local government or electrical, but whilst he lost market share, with volume dropping from 1,700 to 1,300, he was able to invest some of this revenue in developing a range of bearings for the emerging freezing industry, which promised high margins for the future, i.e. an investment in R & D.

The cumulative result of these strategies was that in year 3 he had a volume of 9,400 units, i.e. an increase of over 30 per cent, and a well-balanced portfolio of products. There was also the prospect of new business in Europe from the freezing industry.

This case study demonstrates how the DPM can be constructed and used to good effect. Any organization should be able to follow a similar process to that used by International Bearings. The only contentious point is that a company must be clear about how it defines its markets. Any woolly thinking about these will undermine the value of the DPM and will probably generate some downright misleading information.

Anyone with any doubts about market definition would be well advised to look back at Exercise 4.1.

APPENDIX 1 SOME IMPORTANT INSTRUCTIONS FOR USING THE DIRECTIONAL POLICY MATRIX IN MARKETING PLANNING (EX.5.4)

Business strengths

Table 5.17 is a typical calculation made by an organization to estimate its strength in a market. From this table it will be seen that:

- This organization is not market leader.
- All competitors score above 5.0.

Table 5.17

1 Critical success factors (What are the few key things that any competitor has to do right to succeed?)	2 Weighting (How important is each of these CSFs? Score out of 100.)	3 Strengths/weaknesses analysis (Score yourself and each of your main competitors out of ten on each of the CSFS, then multiply the score by the weight.)				
		CSF/ comp.	You	Comp.A	Comp.B	Comp.C
1 Product	20	1	9=1.8	6=1.2	5–1.0	4=0.8
2 Price	10	2	8=0.8	5=0.5	6=0.6	10=1.0
3 Service	50	3	5=2.5	9=4.5	7=3.5	6=3.0
4 Image	20	4	8=1.6	8=1.6	5=1.0	3=0.6
(These should normally be viewed from the customer's point of view.)	Total 100	Total (score × weight)	6.7	7.8	6.1	5.4

The problem with this and many similar calculations is that rarely will this method discriminate sufficiently well to indicate the relative strengths of a number of products in a particular company's product/market portfolio. Some method, then, is required to prevent all products appearing on the left of the matrix. This can be achieved by using a *ratio*, as in the Boston Matrix referred to earlier in this chapter. In this case, a ratio will indicate a company's position *relative* to the best in the market. In the example provided, Competitor A has most strengths in the market, so our organization probably needs to make some improvements when compared with the 'leader'. To reflect this, our weighted score should be expressed as a *ratio* of Competitor A (the highest weighted score). Thus $6.7 \div 7.8 = 0.86{:}1$. If we were to plot this on a *logarithmic* scale on the horizontal axis, this would place our organization to the *right* of the dividing line, as follows:

$$3\times \qquad 1 \qquad 0.3$$

A scale of 3× to 0.3 has been chosen because such a band is likely to encapsulate most extremes of competitive advantage. If it doesn't, just change it to suit your own industry circumstances.

Market-attractiveness factors

The first time managers try using the directional policy matrix, they frequently find that the circles do not come out where expected. One possible reason for this is a misunderstanding concerning the use of market-attractiveness factors. Please remember, you will be most concerned about the *potential* for *growth in volume, growth in profit*, and so on for your organization in each of your 'markets'. For example, even if a 'market' is mature (or even in decline), if the *potential* is there for your company to grow in this mature market, then it would obviously be more attractive than one in which there was little or no potential for you to grow. (As would be the case, for example, if you already had a high market share.) Likewise, even if a 'market' is currently very profitable for your company, if there was little or no *potential* for growing the profit, this 'market' might be considered less attractive than one which was currently not so profitable to your company, but which offered good *potential* for growing your profits.

Also, in considering the position of the circles at some time in the future, it is important to remember that they can only move *vertically* if the matrix shows the level of attractiveness at the present time. This implies carrying out one set of calculations for the present time according to the agreed market-attractiveness factors, in order to locate markets on the vertical axis, then carrying out another set of calculations for a future period (say, in 3 years' time), based on your forecasts according to the same market-attractiveness factors. In practice, it is quicker and easier to carry out only the latter calculation, in which case the circles can only move horizontally.

Once agreed, under no circumstances should market-attractiveness factors be changed, otherwise the attractiveness of your markets is not being evaluated against common criteria and the matrix becomes meaningless. Scores, however, will be specific to each market.

Please note, however, that you *must* list the 'markets' that you intend to apply the criteria to *before* deciding on the criteria themselves, since the purpose of the vertical axis is to discriminate between more and less attractive 'markets'. This will prevent all your 'markets' appearing in the top half of the matrix, which would clearly make the exercise pointless.

The criteria themselves, therefore, must be specific to the population of 'markets' under consideration, and, once agreed, must not be changed for different 'markets' in the same population.

A word of warning should also be offered at this point. It should be stressed that markets positioned in the lower half of the matrix should not be treated as unattractive. All this means is that they are relatively less attractive than markets positioned in the top half of the matrix.

Another important point about the directional policy matrix is that it can be used not just for markets, but for countries, markets within countries, segments within markets, and outlets within markets. Each time, however, the criteria will obviously be different. It can even be used for agents and distributors. One major chemical company used the directional policy matrix to select fifty distributors out of the 450 it was dealing with. It needed to do this because the market was in decline and the distributors began *buying* for customers rather than *selling* for the supplier. This led to a dramatic fall in prices. The only way the chemical company could begin to tackle the problem was by appointing a number of exclusive distributorships. The issue of which distributorships to choose was tackled using the directional policy matrix, as clearly some were more attractive than others, while the company had varying strengths in their dealings with each distributor.

APPENDIX 2 CRITERIA WHICH CAN BE USED IN ESTABLISHING MARKET ATTRACTIVENESS AND BUSINESS STRENGTHS (EX.5.4)

See Table 5.18.

Table 5.18

Attractiveness of your market	*Status/position of your business*
1 *Market factors*	
Size (money units or both)	Your share (in equivalent terms)
Size of key segments	Your share of key segments
Growth rate per year:	Your annual growth rate:
total	total
segments	segments
Diversity of market	Diversity of your participation
Sensitivity to price, service features and external factors	Your influence on the market
Cyclicality	Lags or leads in your sales
Seasonality	
Bargaining power of upstream suppliers	Bargaining power of your suppliers
Bargaining power of downstream suppliers	Bargaining power of your customers

Table 5.18   Continued

Attractiveness of your market	Status/position of your business
2 *Competition*	
Types of competitors	Where you fit, how you compare
Degree of concentration	in terms of products, marketing
Changes in type and mix	capability, service, production strength, financial strength, management
Entries and exits	Segments you have entered or left
Change in share	Your relative share change
Substitution by new technology	Your vulnerability to new technology
Degrees and types of integration	Your own level of integration
3 *Financial and economic factors*	
Contribution margins	Your margins
Leveraging factors, such as economies of scale and experience	Your scale and experience
Barriers to entry or exit (both financial and non-financial)	Barriers to your entry or exit (both financial and non-financial)
Capacity utilization	Your capacity utilization
4 *Technological factors*	
Maturity and volatility	Your ability to cope with change
Complexity	Depths of your skills
Differentiation	Types of your technological skills
Patents and copyrights	Your patent protection
Manufacturing process technology required	Your manufacturing technology
5 *Sociopolitical factors in your environment*	
Social attitudes and trends	Your company's responsiveness and flexibility
Laws and government agency regulations	Your company's ability to cope
Influence with pressure groups and government representatives	Your company's aggressiveness
Human factors, such as unionization and community acceptance	Your company's relations internally and within the community

Exercise 5.5 Applying the directional policy matrix to your own organization

Follow these instructions:

1   Choose a product (or group of products) that is bought by many different markets (or segments).
2   List no more than eight of these markets (or segments).
3   Develop a set of criteria for judging:

   - Market attractiveness.
   - Your strength in these markets.

4   Develop a scoring and weighting system for these criteria.
5   Evaluate the markets you have chosen, using these criteria.
6   Locate the point of each of these markets on a four-box directional policy matrix.
7   Using an approximate scale of your own choice, make the circle diameter proportional to your current turnover.
8   Comment on the current portfolio.
9   Indicate approximately the size and position of each circle in 3 years' time.
10 Outline (briefly) the strategies you would pursue to achieve these objectives.

For more technical details on the construction of the directional policy matrix, please read pp. 100–110 of *Marketing Plans: how to prepare them; how to use them* (Butterworth Heinemann, 1989).

6 Setting marketing objectives and strategies

> Corporate objective

This is the desired level of profit the organization seeks to achieve. The *corporate strategy* for doing this covers:

1 Which products and which markets (marketing).
2 What facilities are required (e.g. production, distribution).
3 The number and character of employees (personnel).
4 What funding is required and how (finance).
5 Social responsibility, corporate image etc. (other corporate strategies).

> *Gap analysis*

Gap analysis explores the shortfall between the corporate objective and what can be achieved by various strategies.

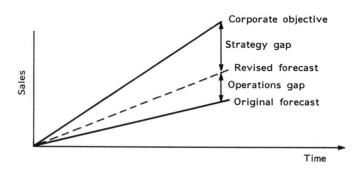

The *operations gap* can be filled by reducing costs, improving the sales mix, increasing market share.

The *strategy gap* can be filled by finding new user groups, entering new segments, geographical expansion, diversification, new product development.

Try Exercise 6.1

The marketing audit

This is the systematic collection of data and information about the external environment and about your own company's operations.

Try Exercise 6.2

The SWOT analysis

This is the summary of the marketing audit, which lists:

Internally
The company's strengths and weaknesses.

Externally
The opportunities and threats facing the company.

The SWOT analysis should provide strong evidence about what the company should and should not try to set as marketing objectives. It should use strengths to exploit opportunities, while minimizing threats and weaknesses.

Try Exercise 6.3, 6.4 and 6.5

Marketing objectives

These are concerned with what is sold (products) and to whom it is sold (markets). There are four possible combinations of products and markets (Ansoff Matrix).

Products

	Existing	New
	Existing	A	B
	New	C	D

Markets

An objective contains three elements:

1 The attribute chosen for measurement, e.g. sales, market share.
2 The particular value selected, e.g. 25 per cent market share.
3 For a given operating period, e.g. by the end of year 3.

The matrix suggests four main categories of objectives:

A = market penetration
B = product development
C = market extension
D = diversification

Try Exercise 6.6

| *Marketing strategies* |

There are four broad strategies:

1 To invest and grow.
2 To extract earnings selectively.
3 To harvest.
4 To divest.

There are also more specific marketing strategies concerning the four Ps

1 *Product*
   - Expand range.
   - Improve quality or features.
   - Consolidate range.
   - Standardize design.
   - Reposition product.
   - Change the mix.
   - Branding.
2 *Price*
   - Change price.
   - Change terms and conditions.
   - Penetration policy.
   - Skimming policy.
3 *Promotion*
   - Change advertising.
   - Change promotion.
   - Change selling.
   - Change communication mix.
4 *Place*
   - Change channels.
   - Change delivery or distribution.
   - Change service levels.
   - Forward or backward integration.

Try Exercise 6.7

| *Questions raised for the company* |

1 Q: Who should set the marketing objectives and strategies?
   A: Usually they would be formulated by the marketing Director, but they must be agreed at the highest level in the company so that there is genuine commitment to them.
2 Q: Is diversification really a viable objective, bearing in mind the risk in moving into the unknown?
   A: It depends how strong the *factual* evidence is for this step. Clearly it is not a decision to be taken lightly.
3 Q: How secret should marketing objectives and strengths be? Should staff at lower levels know what they are?
   A: Staff are much more committed to a company which 'knows

where it is going'. Ideally subordinates should be given the necessary information to understand their job context.

4   Q: What happens if we get our marketing objectives and strategies wrong?

     A: If the process used for arriving at them was based on facts, the chances are they will not be wrong. Clearly it will be essential to monitor progress and take corrective action when required.

Introduction

In this chapter, the most critical part of the marketing planning process will be tackled.

Exercise 6.1 is concerned with carrying out a gap analysis.

Exercise 6.2 is concerned with collecting relevant data about your company and subjecting this to a hard-hitting examination, in summary form, of the opportunities and threats facing your organization.

Exercise 6.3 is concerned with competitor analysis, which clearly is an important part of a marketing audit.

Exercise 6.4 is concerned with carrying out a SWOT analysis.

Exercise 6.5 looks at the assumptions that are made before setting marketing objectives. Clearly, such assumptions should be kept to a minimum, but it is useful to be under no misapprehension regarding what they are, and, just as importantly, the risks attached to making such assumptions.

Exercise 6.6 gets to the heart of the matter and is concerned with setting marketing objectives, while Exercise 6.7 addresses the issue of selecting the most appropriate marketing strategies to match the chosen objectives.

Exercise 6.1   Gap analysis

You are asked to complete this two-part exercise. The first part is concerned with *revenue*, the second with *profit*.

1 REVENUE

Objective

Start by plotting the sales position you wish to achieve at the end of the planning period, point E (Figure 6.1). Next plot the forecast position, point A.

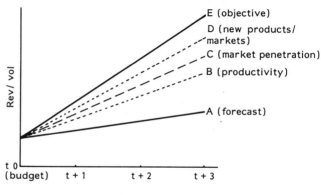

Figure 6.1

Productivity

Are there any actions you can take to close the gaps under the headings in Table 6.1, point B? (These represent cash and margin focus.)

Table 6.1

Productivity (NB: not all factors are mutually exclusive)	Revenue
Better product mix (1)	
Better customer mix (2)	
More sales calls (3)	
Better sales calls (4)	
Increase price	
Reduce discounts	
Charge for deliveries	
TOTAL	

Ansoff product/market (market penetration)

List principal products on the horizontal axis (in Figure 6.2) and principal markets on the vertical axis. In each smaller square write in current sales and achievable sales during the planning period.

Next, plot the market penetration position, point C (Figure 6.1). This point will be the addition of all the values in the right-hand half of the small boxes in the Ansoff matrix. Please note, revenue from (1)(2)(3) and (4) from the productivity box should be deducted from the market penetration total before plotting point C.

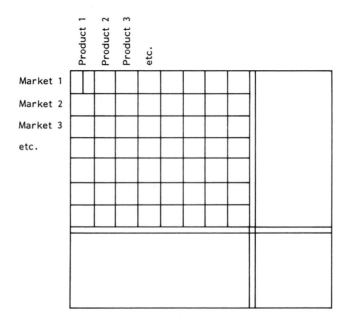

Figure 6.2

Ansoff product/market matrix (new products/new markets)

Next, list the value of any new products you might develop which you might sell to existing markets (Figure 6.3). Alternatively, or as well as, if necessary, list the value of any existing products that you might sell to new markets. Plot the total value of these on Figure 6.1, point D.

Diversification

List the value of any new products you might develop for new markets until point E is reached. (Steps 3, 4 and 5 represent a sales growth focus.)

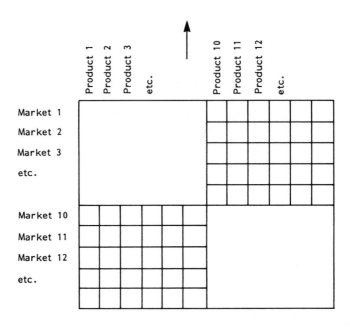

Figure 6.3

Capital utilization
If none of this gives the required return on investment consider changing
the asset base. This could be:

(A) Acquisition
(B) Joint venture

2 PROFIT

Objective
Start by plotting the profit position you wish to achieve at the end of the
planning period, point E (Figure 6.4).
   Next plot the forecast profit position, point A.

Productivity
Are there any actions you can take to close the gap under the headings
in Table 6.2? Plot the total profit value of these in Figure 6.4, point B.
(These represent cash and margin focus.)

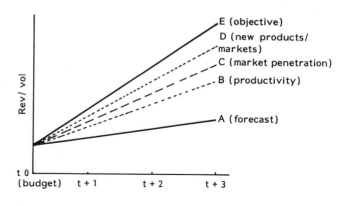

Figure 6.4

Table 6.2

Productivity (NB: not all factors are mutually exclusive)	Profit
Better product mix	
Better customer mix	
More sales calls	
Better sales calls	
Increase price	
Reduce discounts	
Charge for deliveries	
Reduce debtor days	
Cost reduction	
Others (specify)	
Total	

Ansoff product/market (market penetration)

List principal products on the horizontal axis in Figure 6.4 and principal markets on the vertical axis. In each smaller square write in current profit and achievable profit value during the planning period.

Next plot the market penetration position, point C, Figure 6.4. This point will be the addition of all the values in the right-hand half of the small boxes in the Ansoff matrix (Figure 6.5).

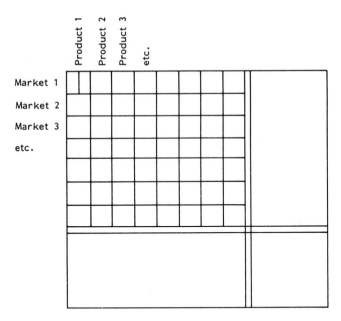

Figure 6.5

Ansoff product/market matrix (new products/new markets)
Next, list the value of any new products you might develop which you
might sell to existing markets (Figure 6.6). Alternatively, or as well as,
if necessary, list the value of any existing products that you might sell to
new markets. Plot the total value of these on Figure 6.3, point D.

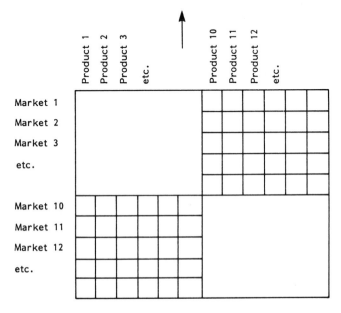

Figure 6.6

Diversification
List the profit value of any new products you might develop for new markets until point E is reached. (Steps 3, 4 and 5 represent a sales growth focus.)
Capital utilization
If none of this gives the required return on investment consider changing the asset base. This could be:

(A) Acquisition
(B) Joint venture

Exercise 6.2 The marketing audit

STAGE 1 COLLECTING THE DATA

All the earlier exercises in this book have been designed to improve your understanding of aspects of marketing planning and to discover information about your company and/or its key products and markets. If you completed all the preceding exercises, you should by now be in possession of a fairly comprehensive marketing audit of your organization. However, since every business is in some ways unique, there is a chance that an important piece of information might have been missed. The marketing audit checklist which follows is provided as a safeguard against this happening.

Use this list to decide if there is any additional information you would want to add to that you have already collected. When you have completed assembling as much information as you can, you are in a position to progress to stage 2 of this exercise.

THE MARKETING AUDIT CHECKLIST

The following is a list of factors that can affect some businesses. You should only be interested in those that will affect your particular business.

This list doesn't claim to be exhaustive but it is intended to provide fair coverage of most areas thereby acting as a guide and stimulus.

EXTERNAL FACTORS
Business and economic environment

Economic	Inflation
	Unemployment
	Energy prices
	Price volatility
Political/	Availability of materials, etc.
fiscal/legal	Nationalization
	Trade unions
	Taxation
	Duties/levies
	Regulatory constraints, e.g. labelling
	quality
	safety etc.
Social/cultural	Demographic issues, e.g. age distribution,
	etc.

	Changes in consumer lifestyle
	Environmental issues, e.g. pollution
	Education
	Immigration/emigration
Technical	Religion, etc.
	New technology/processes
	Energy-saving techniques
	New materials/substitutes
	New equipment
	New products, etc.
Intra-company	Capital investment
	Closures/start-ups
	Strikes, etc.

The market

Total market	Size (value/volume)
	Growth (value/volume)
	Trends (value/volume)
Characteristics	Developments, etc.
Products	Principal products bought
	How they are used
	Where they are used
	Packaging
	Accessories, etc.
Prices	Price levels/range
	Terms and conditions of sale
	Trade practices
	Special discounts
	Official regulations, etc.
Physical distribution	Principal methods
	Batch sizes
	Mechanical handling
	Protection, etc.
Distribution channels	Principal channels
	Purchasing patterns
	Geographical disposition
	Stocks
	Turnover
	Incentives
	Purchasing ability
	Needs
	Tastes
	Profits
	Prices paid, etc.

Customers and consumers	as for Distribution channels plus Demographic considerations, e.g. age, height, etc.
Communications	Principal methods
	Salesforce
	Advertising
	Exhibitions
	Public relations
	Promotions
	New developments, etc.
Industry practices	Inter-firm comparisons
	Trade associations
	Trade regulations/practices
	Links with govt.
	Historical attitudes
	Image, etc.

Competition

Industry structure	The companies in the Industry
	Their make-up
	Their market standing/reputation
	Their capacity to produce
	market
	distribute
	Their diversification
	Their origins and ownership
	New entrants
	Mergers and acquisitions
	Bankruptcies
	International links
	Strengths/weaknesses, etc.
Industry profitability	Historical data
	Current performance
	Relative performance of competitors
	Structure of operating costs
	Level of investment
	Return on investment
	Pricing/volume
	Sources of funding, etc.

INTERNAL FACTORS (OWN COMPANY)

Sales	Total (value/volume)
	by geographical location
	by industry/market segment
	by customer
	by product, etc.

Market share
Profit margins
Marketing
  procedures
Organization
  structure
Sales/marketing
  control data
Marketing mix
  variables

Market research
Product development
Product range
Product quality
Unit of sale
Stock levels
Distribution
Dealer support
Pricing/discounts/credit
Packaging
Samples
Exhibitions
Selling
Sales aids
Point of sale
Advertising
Sales promotion
Public relations
After-sales service
Training and development

Systems and
procedures

Marketing planning system, e.g. is it
  effective?
Marketing objectives, e.g. clear, consistent
  with corporate objectives
Marketing strategy, e.g. appropriate for
  objectives
Structure, e.g. are duties and
  responsibilities clear?
Information, e.g. adequacy of marketing
  intelligence, its presentation
Control, e.g. suitable mechanisms
Communications, e.g. effective? in all areas?
Interfunction efficiency, e.g. between
  functions/departments
Profitability, e.g. regular monitoring and
  analysis

Cost-effectiveness, e.g. are
functions/products continually reviewed
in attempts to reduce excess costs?

STAGE 2 THE SWOT ANALYSIS

From the above list you will see that the *external factors* are the sources
of all opportunities or threats, whereas the *internal factors* reflect the
company's strengths or weaknesses.

In respect of *external factors* (*opportunities and threats*), try the following
exercise:

Step 1 List the principal *opportunities* (we suggest no more than
twenty).

Step 2 Allocate a code to each of these (e.g. A, B, C etc.)

Step 3 Allocate a number between 1 and 9 to each of them. The
number 1 means that in your view there is little chance of a
particular opportunity occurring within the planning time-scale
(say 3 years). A 9 would mean that there is a high probability
of it occurring within the planning time-scale.

Step 4 Allocate a number between 1 and 9 to indicate the importance
of the *impact* each of these opportunities would have on the
organization, were it to occur.

Step 5 Now put each of your *opportunities* on the *opportunities matrix*
(Figure 6.7).

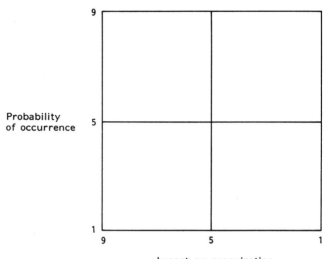

Figure 6.7 *Opportunities matrix*

Step 6 You will now have a number of points of intersection which should correspond to your coding system.

Step 7 All those in the *top left* box should be tackled in your marketing objectives and should appear in your SWOT analysis (Exercise 6.5). All the others, while they should not be ignored, are obviously less urgent. The whole exercise should now be repeated for *threats*, using the matrix in Figure 6.8.

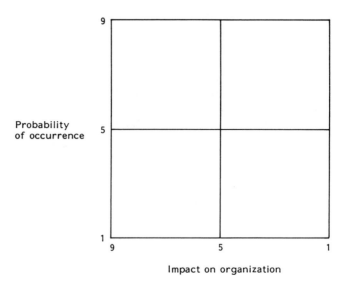

Figure 6.8 *Threats matrix*

Exercise 6.3 Competitor analysis

Exercise 6.3 is concerned with summarizing the information gathered about your opportunities and threats in your marketing audit in a more usable format, in the SWOT analysis.

Before moving on to the SWOT analysis (Exercise 6.4), complete the competitor analysis table (Table 6.3) in order to help you to rate yourself more accurately against your competitors.

Guidelines for completing Table 6.3 are given below.

Table 6.3 **Competitor analysis**

Main competitor	Products/ markets	Business direction and current objectives and strategies	Strengths	Weaknesses	Competitive position

GUIDE TO COMPETITIVE POSITION CLASSIFICATIONS

Leadership	• Has major influence on performance or behaviour of others.
Strong	• Has a wide choice of strategies.
	• Able to adopt independent strategy without endangering short-term position.
	• Has low vulnerability to competitors' actions.
Favourable	• Exploits specific competitive strength, often in a product-market niche.

	• Has more than average opportunity to improve position; several strategies available.
Tenable	• Performance justifies continuation in business.
Weak	• Currently unsatisfactory performance; significant competitive weakness.
	• Inherently a short-term condition; must improve or withdraw.

The following list includes five business directions that are appropriate for almost any business. Select those that best summarize the competitor's strategy.

BUSINESS DIRECTIONS

1 *Enter* – allocate resources to a new business area. Consideration should include building from prevailing company or unit strengths, exploiting related opportunities and defending against perceived threats. It may mean creating a new industry.
2 *Improve* – to apply strategies that will significantly improve the competitive position of the business. Often requires thoughtful product/market segmentation.
3 *Maintain* – to maintain one's competitive position. Aggressive strategies may be required, although a defensive posture may also be assumed. Product/market position is maintained, often in a niche.
4 *Harvest* – to relinquish intentionally competitive position, emphasizing short-term profit and cashflow but not necessarily at the risk of losing the business in the short term. Often entails consolidating or reducing various aspects of the business to create higher performance for that which remains.
5 *Exit* – to divest oneself of a business because of its weak competitive position or because the cost of staying in it is prohibitive, and the risk associated with improving its position is too high.

Exercise 6.4   The SWOT analysis

Having completed the marketing audit, your task now is to summarize it into a cogent and interesting analysis of your company's particular situation. The SWOT approach (the word SWOT incidentally being derived from the initial letters of Strengths, Weaknesses, Opportunities and Threats) will enable you to list in simple terms:

1   Your company's differential strengths and weaknesses *vis-à-vis* competitors.
2   Where the best opportunities exist, i.e. market segments.
3   The present and future threats to your business in the market segments.

The SWOT analysis should only be a few pages in length and should concern itself with key factors only, supported by relevant data.

Some of the most valuable information for the SWOT analysis will come from the life-cycle analysis and the portfolio matrix you prepared in Chapter 5. The former will give you insights about the prospects for your key products and/or services and this information can then be used on the portfolio matrix, thereby highlighting how the portfolio will change. An example of this is shown in Figure 6.9.

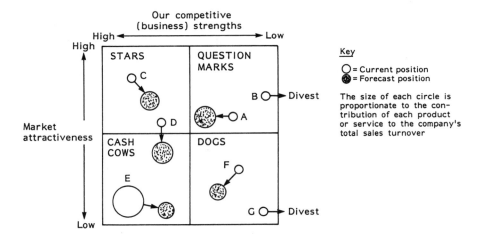

Figure 6.9

In Figure 6.9, clearly the future portfolio is going to be significantly different from the current one. Products/segments B and G will disappear. The sales volume of A, C and D will increase, while that of E will reduce quite dramatically. All this has a tremendous bearing on how funds are generated, and, again, this is where the portfolio matrix can be helpful in letting one understand what is happening. If you recall, the text explained that different quadrants of the matrix had different characteristics when viewed as sources of funds (Figure 6.10).

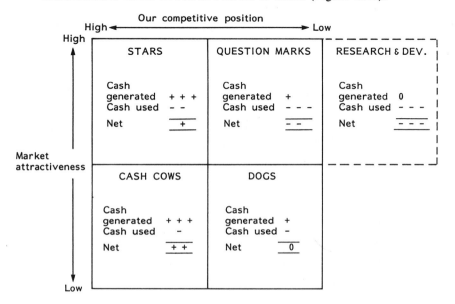

Figure 6.10

The significance of this for any company is to have a balanced portfolio, where there are adequate 'cash cows' to fund research and development and selected 'question marks'.

The effort and costs associated with keeping the market share for 'stars' makes them unreliable sources of funds. The benefits will be reaped later when today's 'stars' sink into the 'cash cow' quadrant.

You can now proceed to complete the proforma provided in respect of *all your key market segments*. Thus, if you have six key market segments, you will complete six proformae. In this book, we have provided you with four forms. If you need more, just repeat the exercise using duplicate forms. See Figures 6.11 to 6.14.

1 SBU description

Here, describe the market for which the SWOT is being done

2 Critical success factors

What are the few key things from the customer's point of view, that any competitor has to do right to succeed?

1

2

3

4

5

3 Weighting

How important is each of these CSFs? Score out of 100

Total 100

4 Strengths/weaknesses analysis

Score yourself and each of your main competitors out of 10 on each of the CSFs. Then multiply the score by the weight

Comp CSF	You	Competitor A	Competitor B	Competitor C	Competitor D
1					
2					
3					
4					
5					
Total (score × weight)					

5 Opportunities/threats

What are the few key things outside your direct control that have had, and will continue to have, an impact on your business?

Opportunities

Threats

1
2
3
4
5

6 Key issues that need to be addressed

152

7

Key assumptions for the planning period

1	
2	
3	
4	
5	
6	
7	

8   *Key objectives*

9   *Key strategies*

Financial consequences

Figure 6.11   *Strategic planning exercise (SWOT analysis)*
Note: This form should be completed for each product/market segment under consideration

1   *SBU description*

Here, describe the market for which the SWOT is being done

2   *Critical success factors*

What are the few key things from the customer's point of view, that any competitor has to do right to succeed?

1	
2	
3	
4	
5	

3   *Weighting*

How important is each of these CSFs? Score out of 100

Total 100

4   *Strengths/weaknesses analysis*

Score yourself and each of your main competitors out of 10 on each of the CSFs. Then multiply the score by the weight

CSF / Comp	You	Competitor A	Competitor B	Competitor C	Competitor D
1					
2					
3					
4					
5					
Total (score × weight)					

5   *Opportunities/threats*

What are the few key things outside your direct control that have had, and will continue to have, an impact on your business?

Opportunities

Threats

6   *Key issues that need to be addressed*

1	
2	
3	
4	
5	

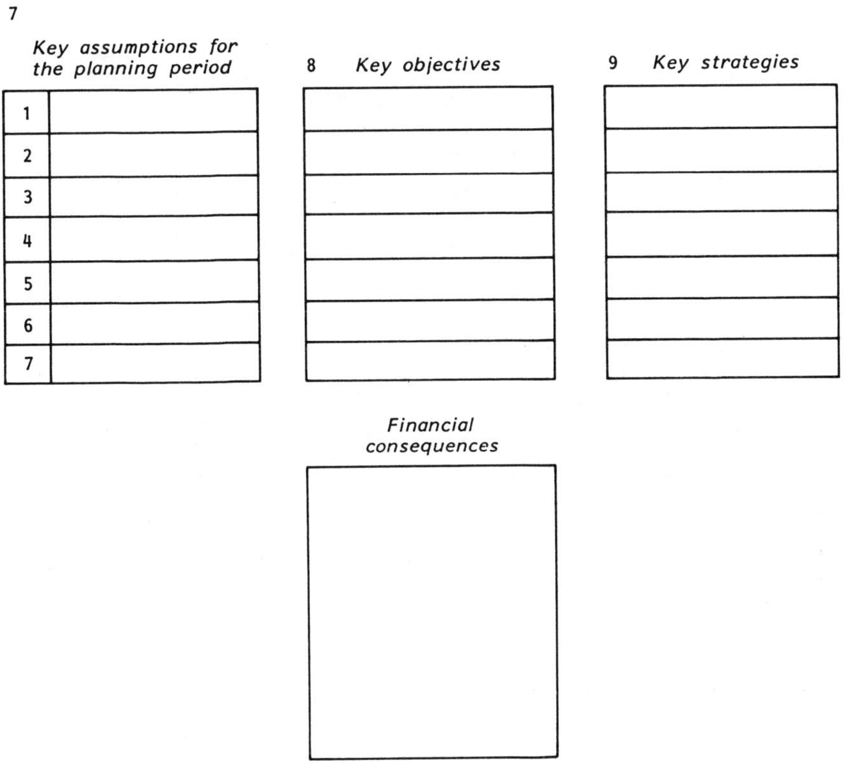

7

Key assumptions for
the planning period

1	
2	
3	
4	
5	
6	
7	

8   Key objectives

9   Key strategies

Financial
consequences

Figure 6.12   *Strategic planning exercise (SWOT analysis)*
Note: This form should be completed for each product/market segment under consideration

1 SBU description

Here, describe the market for which the SWOT is being done

2 Critical success factors

What are the few key things from the customer's point of view, that any competitor has to do right to succeed?

1
2
3
4
5

3 Weighting

How important is each of these CSFs? Score out of 100

Total 100

4 Strengths/weaknesses analysis

Score yourself and each of your main competitors out of 10 on each of the CSFs. Then multiply the score by the weight

Comp CSF	You	Competitor A	Competitor B	Competitor C	Competitor D
1					
2					
3					
4					
5					
Total (score × weight)					

5 Opportunities/threats

What are the few key things outside your direct control that have had, and will continue to have, an impact on your business?

Opportunities

Threats

6 Key issues that need to be addressed

1
2
3
4
5

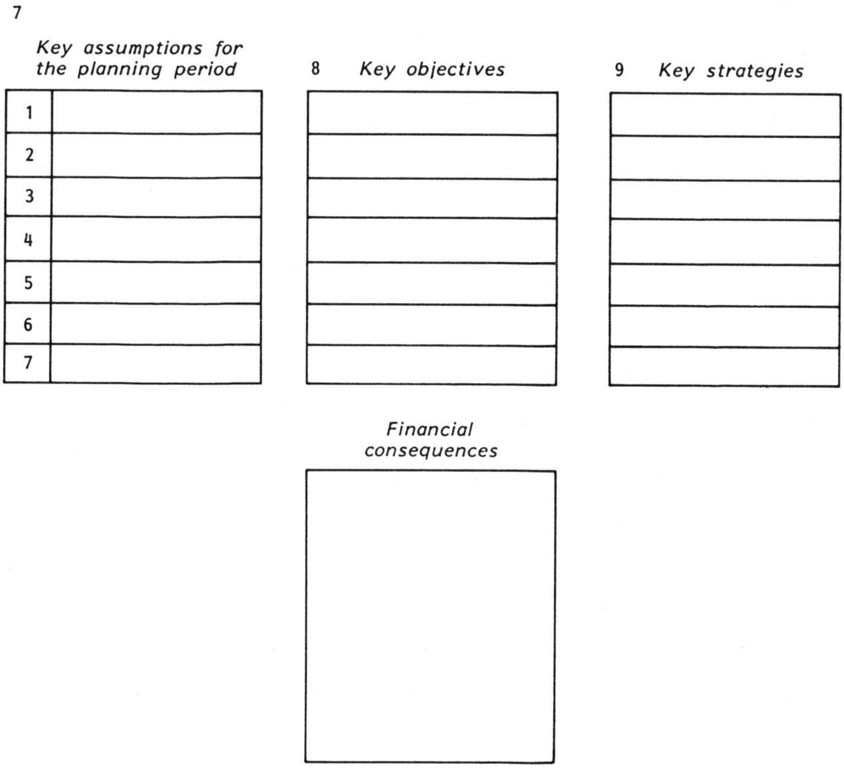

7

Key assumptions for
the planning period

8   Key objectives

9   Key strategies

1	
2	
3	
4	
5	
6	
7	

Financial
consequences

Figure 6.13   *Strategic planning exercise (SWOT analysis)*
Note: This form should be completed for each product/market segment under consideration

1 SBU description

Here, describe the market for which the SWOT is being done

2 Critical success factors

What are the few key things from the customer's point of view, that any competitor has to do right to succeed?

1
2
3
4
5

3 Weighting

How important is each of these CSFs? Score out of 100

Total 100

4 Strengths/weaknesses analysis

Score yourself and each of your main competitors out of 10 on each of the CSFs. Then multiply the score by the weight

CSF \ Comp	You	Competitor A	Competitor B	Competitor C	Competitor D
1					
2					
3					
4					
5					
Total (score × weight)					

5 Opportunities/threats

What are the few key things outside your direct control that have had, and will continue to have, an impact on your business?

Opportunities

1
2
3
4
5

Threats

6 Key issues that need to be addressed

7

Key assumptions for
the planning period   8   Key objectives   9   Key strategies

1	·
2	
3	
4	
5	
6	
7	

Financial
consequences

Figure 6.14   *Strategic planning exercise (SWOT analysis)*
Note: This form should be completed for each product/market segment under consideration

Exercise 6.5 Assumptions

Often it is forgotten that in conducting the SWOT analysis we have had to make assumptions, or educated guesses, about some of the factors that will affect the business, e.g. about market-growth rates, about government economic policy, about the activities of our competitors, etc. Most planning assumptions tend to deal with the environment or market trends and as such are critical to the fulfilment of the planned marketing objectives and strategies.

What then are the risks attached to making assumptions? Suppose we get it wrong?

To give some measure of risk assessment, a technique has been developed that looks at the assumption from the negative point of view. It leads one to ask 'What can go wrong with each assumption that would change the outcome?' For example, suppose the product was an oil derivative and was thus extremely sensitive to the price of oil. For planning purposes an assumption about the price of oil would have to be made. Using this 'Downside Risk' technique we would assess to what level the price could rise before increased material costs would make our products too expensive and cause our marketing plans to be completely revised.

Now complete the following 'Downside risk assessment form' (Table 6.4) to evaluate some of the key assumptions you used in your SWOT analysis, and which you are now to use as the basis for setting marketing objectives and strategies.

Table 6.4 Downside risk assessment form

Key assumption	Basis of assumption	Confidence in assumption high/med/low	What would have to happen to make outcome unattractive?	What is the risk of this happening? High/med/low	What would be impact if event occurs?	How far could things be allowed to deviate from plan before action is taken?	What contingency action is planned?

Exercise 6.6   Setting marketing objectives

The textbook *Marketing Plans: how to prepare them: how to use them* (Butterworth-Heinemann, 1989) goes to some lengths to explain the difference between corporate objectives and marketing objectives. It concludes that marketing objectives are solely concerned with *which products go to which markets*, and that marketing strategies are concerned with *how* that is done. Therefore, because marketing objectives are only concerned about products and markets, an extremely useful planning aid is provided by the Ansoff Matrix, depicted in Figure 6.15.

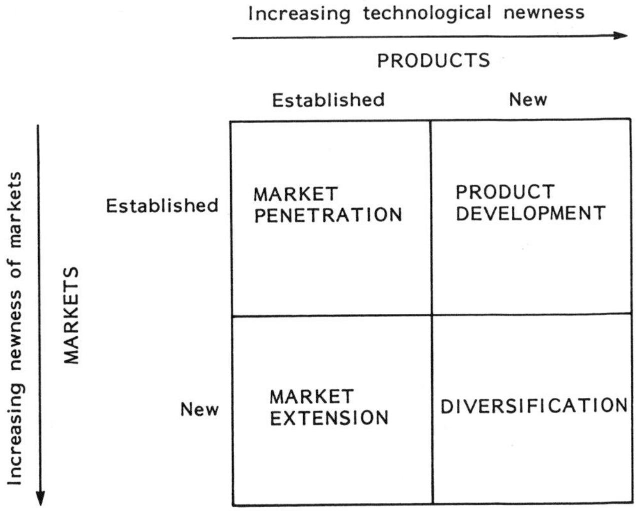

Figure 6.15

This matrix suggests there are four types of marketing objective:

1   Selling established products into established markets (market penetration).
2   Selling established products into new markets (market extension).
3   Selling new products into established markets (product development).
4   Selling new products into new markets (diversification).

Task 1
Using the blank Ansoff Matrix (Figure 6.16), or perhaps using a larger sheet of paper, draw the matrix for your company's products and markets.

Please note that when you consider whether or not a market is new or established, the question you must ask yourself is 'How long does it take to get one's distinctive competence known in this market?' If you have been dealing with the market for anything less than your answer to this question, then that is a new market.

Similarly, new products are those probably at the early stages of their life cycles, where the company is still 'learning' how to make them, i.e. it hasn't solved all the tooling, scheduling, quality, design and technical problems in the same way as it has for the established products.

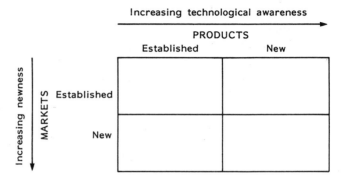

Figure 6.16   *The Ansoff Matrix*

Task 2
Combining the information on the Ansoff Matrix with that of your SWOT analysis, pick out those areas of business that offer the best prospects for your company. For each one summarize your marketing objective for your longer-term planning horizon, i.e. 2, 3, 4 or 5 years. This must be quite explicit in terms of:

(*a*) The product/service.
(*b*) The customer/market segment.
(*c*) The volume of sales.
(*d*) The market share.

Now repeat the exercise, stating the specific objectives for the first year of your planning horizon.

The marketing objectives should be consistent with the information from the product life cycle analysis and portfolio matrix, completed in Chapter 5. Further guidance is provided in the notes which follow.

GUIDELINES FOR SETTING MARKETING OBJECTIVES

Contained within your SWOT analysis will be key information gleaned from your marketing audit. You will know the reasons why customers want your products or services. You will know your best market segments. You will know the 'life' of your products or services and, probably most important of all, the portfolio matrix will have shown you how the various items of your range relate to each other in terms of raising funds.

Creative and intelligent interpretation of the portfolio matrix is the secret behind setting the right marketing objectives for your company. For this to happen, it is important to distinguish the essentially different characteristics of products or services falling into the four quadrants of the matrix. Let us take in turn:

Stars

Products or services in this quadrant are by implication aimed at those markets most attractive to your company. These will almost certainly be the markets with the higher growth rates.

Marketing objectives for such products should be calculated to match or exceed the market-growth rate and thereby hold or extend the company's market share. Since these markets are likely to be attractive to others, the company will have to be aggressive to achieve its objectives. This marketing posture has to be supported by tight budgeting and control processes to ensure that all resources are used effectively. Concern for present earnings should be subordinate to the main thrust of keeping or extending market share.

The increase in sales looked for in these products or services is likely to come from:

1   Possible geographic expansion.
2   Possible product line expansion.
3   Possible product line differentiation.

These may be achieved by internal development, acquisition or joint ventures.

Cash cows

In these less attractive markets it doesn't make sense to go for aggressive growth as with the STARS – it would prove to be too costly and counterproductive. Instead, the objectives should be aimed at maintaining a profitable position with greater emphasis on present earnings.

The most successful products/services should be maintained, while less successful ones should be pruned. Marketing effort should be aimed at maintaining the market share of key market segments with minimum expenditure. Prices should be stabilized except when a temporary aggressive stance is required to maintain market share.

Cash cows must be managed to be the major source of funding for the company.

Question Marks

For products/services in this quadrant there are two broad choices:

(1) Invest in the products for future earnings i.e. groom them to be tomorrow's stars and subsequent cash cows.

or

(2) Manage them for present earnings.

In practice it is only feasible to 'groom' a limited number of question marks and so these have to be carefully chosen for their genuine potential. Investment across the range would be prohibitive.

Dogs

In effect there are two kinds of product/service in this quadrant:

1   Genuine dogs (to the right of the quadrant).
2   Cash dogs (to the left of the quadrant, adjacent to the cash cows).

The marketing objectives for *genuine dogs* should be to divest where appropriate or to manage for present earnings. Marketing expenditure should be minimized, product lines pruned and prices stabilized or raised where possible, even at the expense of sales volume.

The marketing objectives for *cash dogs* should acknowledge the low growth/attractiveness of these products and services, but still seek to identify and exploit growth segments, not by flying in the face of reason and trying to restore the product to its previous higher growth rate by costly advertising and promotion, but by emphasizing product quality and looking for improvements in productivity. Judicious marketing expenditure might be reasonable in special circumstances, but the emphasis should be on maximizing present earnings.

Exercise 6.7 Marketing strategies

Now that the marketing objectives have determined *what* the company must achieve, you have to decide how that might be done by your marketing strategy. Whereas there are only four types of marketing objective, there are a whole range of possible marketing strategies which can be used either singly or in combination with others. A choice of possible marketing strategies is shown in the list below.

Using this list, identify the broad marketing strategies most supportive to each of the marketing objectives you set for the company. Having done this, you will probably find it helpful to refer to the other information, 'Functional Guidelines Suggested by the Portfolio Matrix Analysis' on p. 166 The left-hand column of this chart lists the marketing variables that need to be considered, such as pricing, distribution, etc. The other columns represent the key positions on the portfolio matrix and are headed accordingly. Thus it becomes a fairly straightforward procedure to identify the best marketing strategies for your chosen objectives.

Chapters 7–10 will provide you with additional information about advertising, sales promotion, selling, pricing and distribution. Only finalize your marketing strategies after completing these later sections of this book.

POSSIBLE MARKETING STRATEGIES

1 Change product performance.
2 Change quality or features of product.
3 Change advertising.
4 Change promotion.
5 Change pricing.
6 Change delivery arrangements.
7 Change distribution channels.
8 Change service levels.
9 Improve production efficiency.
10 Improve marketing efficiency.
11 Improve administrative procedures.
12 Change the degree of forward integration.
13 Change the degree of backward integration.
14 Rationalize product range.

15 Withdraw from selected markets.
16 Standardize design.
17 Specialize in certain products/markets.
18 Change sourcing.
19 Buy into new markets.
20 Acquire new/different facilities.
21
22
23
24

Add any other strategies that occur to you in the spaces provided.

FUNCTIONAL GUIDELINES SUGGESTED BY PORTFOLIO MATRIX ANALYSIS

Main thrust	Invest for growth	Maintain market position Manage for earnings	Manage for cash	Prepare for divestment	Opportunistic development
	STAR	CASH COW	CASH DOG	DOG	?
Market share	Maintain or increase dominance	Maintain or slightly milk for earnings	Maintain selectively Segment	Forgo share for profit	Invest selectively in share
Products	Differentiation, line expansion	Prune less successful, differentiate for key segments	Emphasize product quality Differentiate	Aggressively prune	Differentiation, line expansion
Price	Lead Aggressive pricing for share	Stabilize or raise	Maintain or raise	Raise	Aggressive pricing for share
Promotion	Aggressive marketing	Limit	Maintain selectively	Minimize	Aggressive marketing
Distribution	Broaden distribution	Hold wide distribution pattern	Segment	Gradually withdraw distribution	Limited coverage
Cost control	Tight control Go for scale economies	Emphasize cost reduction, viz. variable costs	Tight control	Aggressively reduce both fixed and variable	Tight, but not at expense of entrepreneurship
Production	Expand, invest (organic, acquisition, joint venture)	Maximize capacity utilization	Increase productivity, e.g. specialization, automation	Free up capacity	Invest
R & D	Expand, invest	Focus on specific projects	Invest selectively	None	Invest
Personnel	Upgrade management in key functional areas	Maintain Reward efficiency; tighten organization	Allocate key managers	Cut back organization	Invest
Investment	Fund growth	Limit fixed investment	Invest selectively	Minimize and divest opportunistically	Fund growth
Working capital	Reduce in process, extend credit	Tighten credit, reduce accounts receivable, increase inventory turn	Reduce	Aggressively reduce	Invest

7 Advertising and sales promotion

| The communications mix |

In order to achieve its marketing objectives, the company has to communicate with *existing* and *potential* customers. It can do this *directly*, face to face, generally using a salesforce, or *indirectly*, using advertising, promotion and point of sale displays. The choice of communications mix should be determined on the basis of what is going to be most cost-effective in terms of achieving objectives, i.e. whatever gets the best results per given cost. We will look at direct communication in the next chapter.

| Advertising objectives |

There are many possible advertising objectives:

- to convey information,
- to alter perceptions,
- to alter attitudes,
- to create desires,
- to establish connections, e.g. egg and bacon,
- to direct actions,
- to provide reassurance,
- to remind,
- to give reasons for buying,
- to demonstrate,
- to generate enquiries.

Try Exercises 7.1 and 7.2

Acid test
Is it possible to achieve this objective by advertising alone?

No – rethink objective and/or the means of achieving it.
Yes – go ahead.

The advertising plan

The advertising plan has a number of questions to ask:

- Who is the target audience? What do we know about them? What sort of people are they? etc.
- What response do we want to achieve? What do we want to say, convey, make them feel, believe or understand, etc.?
- How are we going to proceed? What is our creative platform? Can we be sure this is appropriate?
- Where is the best place to put our communications? Will it be cost-effective? Does it generate the right image, etc?

Try Exercise 7.3

- When will our communications be displayed? Is this the best time? Does it mesh in with other activities, etc.?
- Result – what do we expect to achieve? How will we measure this? Does it mesh in with other activities, etc.?
- Budget – how much is needed? How much is going to be available? How will it be controlled, etc.?
- Schedule – who is going to do what, where and when? What is being spent on what, where and when?

Try Exercise 7.4

Sales promotion objectives

Sales promotion seeks to influence:

- salespeople to sell
- customers to buy   more,
- customers to use   earlier,
- users to buy   faster,
- users to use   etc.
- distributors to stock

It is essentially a short-term tactic. In order to achieve these objectives the promotion can use:

Money – price reductions, coupons, competitions, etc.
Goods – free goods, e.g. two for the price of one, trade-ins, free trials, redeemable coupons, etc.
Services – guarantees, training, prizes for events, free services, etc.

Try Exercise 7.5

> *The sales promotion plan*

The sales-promotion plan covers:

- The objectives of the promotion.
- Background – why the method was chosen.
- Eligibility – who and where?
- Timing – opening and closing dates.
- Support in terms of materials.
- Administration required.
- The sales plan – target, incentives.
- Sales presentation – points to cover.
- Monitoring procedure to collect data regarding progress, etc.
- Assessment – how will it be evaluated?

Try Exercise 7.6

> *Questions raised for the company*

1 Q: Who should design the advertising?
   A: There is no golden rule and options might be limited by the available budget. Most companies use outside agencies in order to achieve the required level of professionalism. Advertising objectives, however, should *always* be set by you and *not* by an advertising agency.

2 Q: It's been said that 'half the advertising budget is wasted; the problem is to know which half'. Is this true?
   A: It might be for some companies, but, by following the notes and exercises provided here, you should be able to avoid such a problem.

3 Q: Sales promotions aren't used in our business, so would they be a viable marketing tactic for us?
   A: If, by using a promotion, a company breaks new ground, it could give it a differential advantage over competitors.

4 Q: If a sales promotion is successful, should it be kept running?
   A: Once it has achieved its objectives, there seems little point in continuing. It can always be brought back later, and thereby retain its impact and 'freshness'.

Introduction

This chapter looks at these topics in the context of a 'communications mix'.

It starts with an examination of what advertising objectives are (Exercise 7.1).

It then goes on to look at how to set advertising objectives for one of your own product/market areas (Exercise 7.2), how to choose the most appropriate advertising media (Exercise 7.3) and how to build up an advertising plan (Exercise 7.4).

Sales promotion is tackled in a slightly different way. The first question that is asked is: 'Is a promotion necessary?' (Exercise 7.5). If the answer to this question is affirmative, then Exercise 7.6 demonstrates how to plan a sales promotion.

Exercise 7.1 What are advertising objectives?

There are two basic questions that advertising objectives should address. 'Who are the people we are trying to influence?' and 'What specific benefits or information are we trying to communicate to them?'

Research has shown that many companies set objectives for advertising which advertising cannot possibly achieve on its own. For example, 'to increase sales' or 'to wipe out the competition'. Equally, it is unrealistic to set for an objective 'to convince the target market that our product is best', when any rational analysis would clearly show this not to be true.

Often there is an element of confusion about what advertising objectives are and what marketing objectives are. Remember, marketing objectives are concerned with what products go to which markets, whereas advertising objectives are measurable targets concerned principally with changing attitudes and creating awareness.

Here is a list of marketing objectives and advertising objectives mixed up together. Read through this list and write against each objective:

A – if you believe it to be an advertising objective, or
M – if you believe it to be a marketing objective.

MARKETING (M) OR ADVERTISING (A) OBJECTIVES?*

1　To make attitudes more favourable to a particular product.
2　To build an image for the product.
3　To stop existing users turning to competitive products.
4　To get across the idea of a unique product.
5　To create a brand leader to help the launch of additional products at a future date.
6　To win back previous product users who have defected to a competitive product.
7　To expand the whole market.
8　To reduce existing negative attitudes.
9　To keep building loyalty.
10　To establish the brand and position it in a particular way, e.g. as warm and friendly.

* Based on a list provided by Professor David Corkindale (formerly of Cranfield School of Management) and used with his kind permission.

11 To create a brand leader in a particular market.
12 To increase sales among existing users.
13 To improve the frequency of purchase.
14 To keep new entrants out of the market.
15 To convey the idea that the product is 'value for money'.
16 To say how much people like the product.
17 To improve market share compared with competitors.
18 To maintain brand distribution.

The answers to Exercise 7.1 are as follows:

Advertising objectives: numbers 1, 2, 4, 8, 9, 10, 15 and 16.
Marketing objectives: numbers 3, 5, 6, 7, 11, 12, 13, 14, 17 and 18.

If you made some mistakes in identifying the objectives correctly, go back and have another look at them and see if you can work out where you went wrong. If you can't, read Chapter 7 of *Marketing Plans: how to prepare them; how to use them* (Heinemann 1989).

Exercise 7.2 Setting advertising objectives

Behind all effective advertising there lies a lot of careful thought and planning, and much of it goes into ensuring that the advertising objectives are the right ones. If these are wrong, everything else which follows is doomed to failure.

In this exercise you are asked to concentrate on just one key market or market segment. It should be a relatively simple matter to repeat the process for other markets at some later date.

Make a note somewhere about which market or segment you will be addressing. Remember, from the Boston Matrix or directional policy matrix, 'stars' will probably be most deserving of the advertising budget.

Now make a note about the marketing objectives which have been set for this market/segment, e.g. what products? what quantities? to whom? etc. Having assembled this information, from the list of 'Possible advertising objectives' below:

1   Select the most appropriate objectives, i.e. those that look the most promising to help the company achieve these marketing objectives (tick in the column).
2   From those you have ticked, eliminate any objectives that you believe can *only* be achieved by personal communication, i.e. by the salesforce.
3   List your remaining objectives in rank order, the most important being at the top of the list.
4   Use only the top objective (and perhaps the second) as a basis for your advertising campaign.

POSSIBLE ADVERTISING OBJECTIVES

	Tick here		*Tick here*
• To establish an immediate sale		• To promote the idea of a unique product	
• To bring a prospect closer to a sale		• To back up promotions	
• To change customer perceptions		• To develop favourable attitudes to a particular product	
• To direct customer action		• To counter price competition	
• To support the salesforce		• To remind customers about our product	
• To reinforce attitudes of existing customers		• To reinforce the company image	
• To open up distribution		• To defend market position	
• To improve company image		• To support the launch of a new product/service	
• To demonstrate the product capabilities		• To explain new uses for product	
• To generate enquiries		• To emphasize range and choice	
• To impart information		• To reinforce brand recognition	
• To reassure customers		• To inform about product availability	
• To 'score points' off competitors' advertising		• To educate customers	
• To enter new markets		• To communicate company strengths	
• To give reasons for buying		• To build customer loyalty	
• To create awareness		• To say how much people like the product	
• To support retailers			
• To convey the idea of 'value for money'			
• To reach new geographical areas			

If you think this list omits possible advertising objectives for your company, then extend the list by adding your possibilities to it.

Exercise 7.3 Choosing the advertising media

The previous exercise should have helped to identify the advertising objectives for your chosen market/segment. The next logical step would be to decide exactly what you want to communicate – your creative platform.

However, such a step does not really lend itself to an exercise. Indeed, copywriting is such a specialized form of communication that most companies engage outside specialists to deal with it. Even so, having decided upon the advertising objectives, you must switch your focus of attention now to the target population you hope to influence:

- Who are they?
- What positions do they hold?
- What is their influence on the purchasing decision?
- What personality traits do they exhibit?
- What socioeconomic groupings do they belong to?
- What lifestyles do they have?
- How old are they? What sex are they? Are they married? and so on.

Please note that it is usually easier to determine the most appropriate media in the case of *industrial* customers, although the same logic applies.

You need to assemble as much information as you can about the target population. The more you know about them, the better your chances of selecting the best medium for your advertising platform.

The accompanying worksheet gives a list of possible advertising media. Study this list and select what would be the best choice, taking into account your objectives and the profile of the target audience.

In making your choice, you will need to take four factors into account:

1 *The character of the medium* – the geographical coverage it gives, the types of audience it reaches, its frequency of publication or showing, its physical possibilities (such as colour, sound, movement), its power or potential to reach special groups, etc.
2 *The atmosphere of the medium* – its ability to convey an image consistent with your objectives, e.g. hard and punchy, discreet, elegant, exclusive, etc.
3 *The 'size' of the medium* – the number of people exposed to the medium in terms of being aware of the contents. For example, a

newspaper might be read by two or three members of a family, whereas a technical journal might be circulated to a large number of managers within a company. Alternatively, a poster might be passed by tens of thousands of people.

4   *The comparative cost* – how much will it cost to reach a specific audience. The cost per 1,000 viewers is often used as a comparative ratio.

There is space on the accompanying worksheet to make notes about these factors, should you be required to keep a record of what influenced your choice of medium.

WORKSHEET   Advertising media (Ex. 7.3)

	Medium	Characteristics	Atmosphere	Size	Comparative cost
Printed media	Local newspapers				
	National newspapers				
	Trade and technical press				
	Magazines and periodicals				
	Direct mail				
	Leaflets				
	Directories (Yellow Pages, buyers' guides, etc.)				
Others	Television				
	Posters (static)				
	Transport (on trains, buses, vans, etc.)				
	Cinema				
	Radio				
	Other (specify)				

Exercise 7.4 The advertising plan

Having decided what you want to communicate (your advertising objectives, Exercise 7.1), worked out the creative platform of the exact message you wish to convey, and decided on the choice of media (Exercise 7.2), you have assembled the key ingredients of an advertising plan. What remains to be done is to establish when the advertising will be used, who will be responsible for the various activities in bringing what is still an idea into life, how progress will be monitored and the criteria by which success will be judged.

The accompanying worksheet provides a simple format to record all this information. We would recommend that you try using it, and then adapt it to your particular purposes, so that you finish up with something that is genuinely tailor-made.

WORKSHEET   Advertising plan (Ex. 7.4)

ADVERTISING PLAN FOR _____ (either product or service/market or segment)

ADVERTISING OBJECTIVES TO _____

Selected media	Brief description of advert	Timing	Responsibility	Budget	Actual cost	Criteria by which success will be judged	Evaluation comments

Note. Now complete advertising plans for other products/services and market segments.

Exercise 7.5 Is a promotion necessary?

Sales promotions should be seen as the logical development of the company's marketing strategy. As such, they should be complementary to all other parts of the communications mix and should not be seen as an alternative, or some disconnected activity.

There are three key questions to be answered.

1 How do we decide whether or not to run a promotion?
2 What form should the promotion take?
3 How do we plan it?

The first two questions are addressed by this exercise. The planning element is covered in Exercise 7.6.

In order to give this exercise a clear focus, please select just one of the product/market areas of your portfolio and work with it. Once you have worked through this process, you will see how it can be used elsewhere, with other products/markets.

Step 1 On a separate piece of paper, write down the problems you see affecting sales of the product or service in the market/market segment you have chosen. If there are no problems, you might question why a sales promotion is being considered in this area. Your efforts might be better spent focusing on another part of your product/service range.

Step 2 Look at the problems you have listed and rank them in order of 'seriousness', 1 being the major problem, 2 the next, and so on.

Step 3 Transfer the information you have just assembled to column 1 of the accompanying Worksheet 1.

Step 4 Taking the major problem first, work across the page on the worksheet and consider the possible solutions to the problem listed there. You will note that there is space to add solutions of your own.

Clearly, a sales promotion is not always going to be the way to resolve a sales problem. However, the economics or convenience of one type of solution compared with another might well sway the argument. For example, the best solution to the sales problem might be to modify the product, but this might be very costly and take time to achieve. In such circumstances, a sales promotion might work in terms of both costs and immediacy.

Therefore considered judgement has to be used in weighing up the costs and likely chances of success of each possible solution. *Only* when the sales-promotion option looks favourable should you take matters to the next stage of deciding upon the type of promotion.

Step 5 If a sales promotion will not make any impact on the major sales problem, work across the page again for the next problem down. Continue this process for other sales problems until a sales promotion is found which would appear to hold the promise of success.

Ideally the sales promotion should make impact on a fairly serious sales problem. If it is only going to affect a marginal issue, it raises questions about whether or not it is worth spending the time and effort on the promotion and whether another area might be more deserving of attention.

WORKSHEET 1   Deciding if sales promotion will help (Ex. 7.5)

	Problems affecting sales	POSSIBLE SOLUTIONS												
		More advertising?		More sales effort?		Change price?		Change product?		Sales promotion?		Other ideas (add your own)			
		Cost	Likely success	Cost	Likely success	Cost	Likely success	Cost	Likely success	Cost	Likely success	Cost	Likely success	Cost	Likely success
Major problem	1														
	2														
Problems listed in reducing order	3														
	4														
	5														

PRODUCT/SERVICE/MARKET SEGMENT
UNDER CONSIDERATION _____

Having established that a sales promotion is a suitable way to have an impact on a particular sales problem, you must now decide on the nature of the promotion.

In broad terms, a promotion can be aimed at three target groups:

1   Customers or consumers.
2   Channels/intermediaries.
3   Your own salesforce.

The promotion can also take one of three forms:

1   It can involve money.
2   It can involve goods.
3   It can involve services.

You will have to decide first of all which target group needs to be influenced most to make impact on your sales problem. You might even decide it is more than one group.

Having made that decision, you then have to work out what type of promotion will have maximum appeal to that group. Ideally, you will be able to devise something with maximum appeal, at a modest cost. However, when considering the cost element, you must remember that the promotional costs have to be weighed up against the benefits of reducing the specific sales problem.

Worksheet 2 provides a number of ideas about sales promotions and enables you to select the most appropriate type for your purposes.

WORKSHEET 2   Types of sales promotion (Ex. 7.5)

Target market \ Type of promotion	Money		Goods		Service	
	Money		**Goods**		**Service**	
	Direct	Indirect	Direct	Indirect	Direct	Indirect
Consumer	Price reduction	Coupons Vouchers Money equivalents Competitions	Free goods Premium offers (e.g. 13 for 12) Free gifts Trade in offers	Stamps Coupons Vouchers Money equivalents Competitions	Guarantees Group participation events Special exhibitions and displays	Cooperative advertising Stamps, coupons Vouchers for services Event admissions Competitions
Trade	Dealer loaders Loyalty schemes Incentives Full range Buying schemes	Extended credit Delayed invoicing Sale or return Coupons Vouchers Money equivalents	Free gifts Trial offers Trade in offers	Coupons Vouchers Money equivalents Competitions	Guarantees Group participation events Free services Risk reduction schemes Training Special exhibitions and displays Demonstrations Reciprocal trading schemes	Stamps, coupons Vouchers for services Competitions
Sales-force	Bonus Commission	Coupons Vouchers Points systems Money equivalents Competitions	Free gifts	Coupons Vouchers Points systems Money equivalents	Free services Group participation events	Coupons Vouchers Points systems for services Event admissions Competitions

Exercise 7.6 Planning a sales promotion

It is important to ensure that any sales promotion is well coordinated in terms of what happens before, during and after the promotion. At different stages, different people might be participating and special resources might be required. Therefore a plan needs to be prepared in a simple way that most people can follow. In essence, this is all you need in a plan.

Heading	Content
Introduction	Briefly summarize the problem upon which the promotion is designed to make impact
Objectives	Show how the objectives of the promotion are consistent with the marketing objectives
Background	Provide the relevant data or justification for the promotion
Promotional offer	Briefly, but precisely, provide details of the offer
Eligibility	Who is eligible? Where?
Timing	When is the offer available?
Date plan	The dates and responsibilities for all elements of the promotion
Support	Special materials, samples, etc. that are required by the salesforce, retailers, etc.
Administration	Budgets, storage, invoicing, delivery, etc.
Sales plan	Briefing meetings, targets, incentives, etc.
Sales presentation	Points to be covered
Sales reporting	Any special information required
Assessment	How the promotion will be evaluated

Using these guidelines, and the accompanying worksheet, try to extend the information you assembled in Exercise 7.5 into a complete promotional plan.

WORKSHEET Promotion plan (Ex. 7.6)

	Heading	Content
1	Introduction	
2	Objectives	
3	Background	
4	Promotional offer	
5	Eligibility	
6	Timing	
7	Date plan	
8	Support	
9	Administration	
10	Sales plan	
11	Sales presentation	
12	Sales reporting	
13	Assessment	

8 The sales plan

What is the role of personal selling?

This provides the face-to-face element of the communications mix. There are things it can achieve that advertising and promotion can't, e.g. sales people can be flexible in front of the customer and ask for an order. However, personal selling has to be seen in the context of the total communication mix.

Try Exercise 8.1

How important is personal selling?

Traditionally, companies had salesforces long before marketing was in vogue. Companies still spend more on salesforces than on advertising and promotion combined. Though key parts of the marketing mix, sales departments often act independently of marketing. Thus, in achieving their short-term sales goals, they sometimes fail to achieve the mix of products and markets consistent with the longer-term strategic marketing objectives.

How many sales people should you have?

Basically salespeople have three activities. They:

- make calls,
- travel,
- administrate.

Their workload should be analysed to establish how many calls it is possible to make in a typical working day. Equally, an assessment of existing and potential customers should be made and the annual total number of calls calculated (bear in mind different customer categories need different call rates).

Size of business

	Large	Medium	Small
Friendly	1	2	3
Average	4	5	6
Hostile	7	8	9

Customer attitude

Boxes 1 + 2 = maintenance call rate
Boxes 4 + 5 = increase effort
Boxes 3 + 6 = minimum attention
Boxes 7 + 8 = new strategy
Box 9   = don't bother

Number of salespeople equals:

$$\frac{\text{Annual total calls required}}{\text{Number of working days} \times \text{Cs}}$$

where Cs = all salespeople's calls per day.

What should they do?

Achieve objectives consistent with the marketing plan in terms of:

- How much to sell (volume).
- What to sell (mix).
- Where to sell (market segments).
- Allowable costs.
- Profit margins.

There can be many other types of sub or enabling objectives, e.g.

- Number of telephone contacts.
- Number of sales letters written.
- Number of calls made.
- Use of sales aids.
- Number of reports submitted.
- Safety record, etc.

Try Exercise 8.2

| *How are they managed?* |

To maximize performance, get the optimal balance between incentives and disincentives. Incentives are:

- Rewards consistent with performance.
- Giving praise and recognition where it is due.
- Minimal boredom and monotony.
- Freedom from fear and worry.
- Feeling of belonging.
- Sense of doing a useful job.

'There are no bad sales people, only bad sales managers.'

Try Exercise 8.3

| *Questions raised for the company* |

1 Q: Should sales or marketing be responsible for the sales plan?
   A: Marketing objectives should be agreed first. Then, if there is a separate salesforce, sales managers can devise a tactical plan to meet the objectives.
2 Q: Salespeople are sometimes described as notoriously reactive and optimistic. Can they be expected to conform to a sales plan?
   A: Salespeople such as the ones described here are perhaps the salespeople you don't need. The sales plan is designed to make best use of a scarce and expensive resource, a wholly admirable objective. It must not be undermined.
3 Q: Suppose the sales plan requires salespeople to play a different role. Can 'old dogs' be taught new tricks?
   A: Whenever change is introduced, there are often some casualties. However, with well-designed training and sensitive management the problem is not insurmountable.

Introduction

While it is quite possible that some companies will not use advertising and sales promotion, very few fail to have some element of face-to-face selling in their marketing mix. Often the salesforce was in existence long before the company became concerned about marketing. This sometimes explains why in many organizations, sales and marketing are regarded as two separate functions.

When the total cost of recruiting, managing and providing salespersons with all the necessary resources and support systems is taken into account, the salesforce is likely to be one of the most costly elements of the company's marketing activities. In order to obtain value for money, it will be important to plan how personal selling will be integrated into the 'communications mix', then organize the logistics to ensure that the right results are achieved.

Exercise 8.1 looks at how the role of the salesforce can be established.

Exercise 8.2 tackles the task of how to set quantifiable objectives for the salesforce.

Exercise 8.3 examines issues about managing the salesforce and, in particular, how to set the right motivational climate.

Exercise 8.1 The role of personal communication in the communications mix

Before attempting to produce a sales plan, we must spend a few minutes getting back to basics and examining exactly what information customers will require from the salesforce.

For different sorts of businesses, the role of the salesperson can be entirely different. In some they will just be order-takers, in others negotiators, in others demonstrators, and in others perhaps a composite of these and still other roles. Clearly, then, to claim that a salesperson 'just sells' is very much an oversimplification of the role, and sometimes can be downright misleading.

Taking your marketing objectives as the starting point, i.e. which products/services go to which markets or segments, select one of your key markets/segments as a study vehicle and focus on the customers. What sort of information do they require from your salesforce?

The next worksheet is designed to help you with this task. There are three steps to be tackled:

1 Establish the communication areas that need to be covered.
2 Because of the costs of having a salesforce, assess if there are less costly feasible alternatives to personal visits to achieve the same results.
3 List what these alternatives are, together with when and how they will be used.

Thus on completion of the worksheet you will have a complete breakdown of the personal communications necessary to achieve the company's marketing objectives in your study market segment. In addition, you will have other information to show how personal visits can be 'backed up', using other methods of contact.

WORKSHEET **What information do customers want from sales representatives?**
(Ex. 8.1)

For study purposes, just consider *one* market segment. You can repeat the same procedure for the others afterwards.

Recognizing that the salesforce plays an important part in the company's communication mix, study the list below and then tick those activities 'demanded' by customers in column A. Now look carefully at the activities you have just ticked, and, taking each in turn, ask yourself if this information/communication could be provided in a more efficient way than by a sales visit. For example, knowing the customer usage of a particular product might make it possible to obtain repeat orders by telephone.

Wherever you see the possibility of an alternative approach, place a tick in column B and make a brief note about the alternative.

Customer info. requirement	A	B	Alternative provision of information

About:
 	
product range
product performance
price
discounts
special offers
promotions
placing order
after-sales service
running cost in use
guarantees
spares and accessories
new developments
competitor products/
    performance
assistance with
    displays
assistance with
    merchandising
training for own
    staff
technical services
quality assurance
proof that product/
    service works
warehousing/
    storage
reordering
load sizes
leasing
    agreement
 	
delivery
    arrangements
franchise
    agreement
answers to
    objections
joint ventures			

Customer info. requirement	A	B	Alternative provision of information
demonstration of product long-term contracts financial arrangements Add any other information requirements that are pertinent to your business			

Exercise 8.2 Quantifiable objectives

Having decided what role the salesforce is to play in the communications mix to service your chosen market segment, you can now get down to drawing up some quantifiable objectives. These stem quite logically from the marketing objectives and should cover three main areas:

1 How much to sell (value of unit sales volume).
2 What to sell (the mix of product lines).
3 Where to sell (the markets/segments that take the company towards its marketing objectives).

Please note that in Exercise 8.1, you have already chosen one component, 'where to sell', by selecting an important market or segment.

The sales plan is in effect the translation of these 'ball park' figures into individual targets for each sales representative, taking into account special factors such as their territory size, the size of customers within a particular territory, etc. Thus how much to sell breaks down into individual targets. The mix of the product lines becomes an individual target. Where to sell becomes a specific customer list.

In addition, there can be other quantifiable objectives, typical examples of which are given on the worksheet on p.192. Using this worksheet, you will be able to devise a set of targets appropriate for each of your sales representatives.

If you use one sheet per person, the total will become the sales plan for this particular market segment.

The example on page 193 shows how the basic targeting can be made somewhat more elaborate if it suits your company to make it so.

WORKSHEET   **Individual sales targets** (Ex. 8.2)

Market segment   ....

Salesperson   ....

Territory   ....

Period to which these
targets apply, e.g. year,
month, week, call cycle, etc. ....

Target	Number	Qualifying notes (assumptions, special local factors, etc.)

Unit sales volume
   Product A
   Product B
   Product C
   Product D		

Number of calls planned to be made		
Number of interviews to be secured		
Number of enquiries to be raised		
Number of quotations to be submitted		
Number of orders to be taken		
Call/interview ratio*		
Interview/enquiries ratio*		
Enquiries/quotations ratio*		
Quotations/order ratio*		
Cost per visit		
Calls per day planned		
Average length of call		
Average daily mileage		
Number of new accounts planned		
Number of letters to be written		
Number of reports to be written		
Number of point of sale displays to be organized		
Number of meetings to be held, e.g. with trade		
Number of service calls to be made		

*based on past experience and future
 expectations.

Worksheet   (cont.)

Target	Number	Qualifying notes (assumptions, special local factors, etc.)
Number of customer complaints		
Number of customer training sessions to be run		
Number of competitor activity reports to be submitted		
Number of general market condition reports to be submitted		
Add any others that are relevant to your type of business		

Exercise 8.3   Managing the salesforce

Although some purists might claim this is an oversimplification, the key *management* activities are:

- Setting performance standards (both quantifiable and qualitative).
- Monitoring achievements against these standards.
- Helping/training those who are falling behind.
- Setting the right motivational climate.

The word 'management' has been emphasized because many sales managers perceive themselves to be 'super' salespeople and continue to put most of their energies into selling rather than managing.

SETTING PERFORMANCE STANDARDS

Exercise 8.2 concentrated on the quantifiable standards – *what* has to be achieved. Equally important are the more subjective elements of *how* the tasks are achieved: the quality of the actions.

Some companies have quite deliberately set out to create a style to which salespeople are expected to conform. This can cover appearance (of person and his property), the layout of letters and reports, the way work is planned, the way customers are addressed and various other aspects of the work. You might have to give some consideration to this question of 'the way we do things around here'. But please note that in the examples given above, there is a standard to work against and performance is therefore measurable.

Place less emphasis on non-measurable factors, such as creativity, loyalty, interest, enthusiasm – relying on them too heavily is to plant the seeds of discord. Such subjective judgements can easily be misconstrued as favouritism by some and unfairness by others who have been 'scored' lower. Nonetheless, they can be relevant, so we have included a way of 'measuring' these elements in this exercise.

MONITORING PERFORMANCE

What salespeople are doing can be largely measured by reports, sales figures, internal memos and suchlike. *How* they do things can in most cases only be assessed by being with them and observing their actual performance.

Thus performance will have to be monitored at these two levels, and the frequency for doing so will depend upon the experience of the salesperson, the newness of the operation and the uncertainty of the situation. As a rule of thumb, the higher the uncertainty surrounding the salesperson, the territory, the product range, the customers etc., the more frequently should performance be monitored. The appraisal summary (worksheet 1) provided will enable you to monitor and 'measure' all the relevant quantitative and qualitative elements of your salesforce.

HELPING/TRAINING THOSE WHOSE PERFORMANCE IS BELOW PAR

By having measurable standards of performance, it becomes possible to be quite precise about the area and nature of help that salespeople need. After discussing the problem with them, you will be able to decide if it can be best solved by providing the salespeople with:

- More information (about products, prices etc.).
- More support (typing, more joint visits, etc.).
- More training (which generally means improving their skills).

Often training, which can be the most costly solution, is rushed into when other actions would serve the purpose more effectively.

Should training be required, much of it can be carried out on the job by a suitable skilled instructor, who would follow a process like this:

1 Instruction/demonstration by instructor.
2 Practice by the salesperson.
3 Feedback by the instructor.
4 Further practice with feedback until performance is acceptable.

SETTING THE RIGHT MOTIVATIONAL CLIMATE

Perhaps little of the above will really work unless the motivation of the salesforce is right. While this subject could be the basis of a whole book by itself, it is possible to see a fairly straightforward way of cutting through much of the theoretical undergrowth.

By and large, if you can reduce those factors which tend to demotivate your staff and at the same time accentuate those which motivate them, then the motivational climate must improve. In saying this, it is important

WORKSHEET Individual appraisal summary (Ex. 8.3)

SALESPERSON _____

DIVISION _____

TERRITORY _____ YEAR _____

MANAGER _____

Note:
Score between 5 and 1, when 5 represents excellent and 1 represents poor.

Salesmanship	JAN	FEB	MAR	APR	MAY	JUN	JUL	AUG	SEP	OCT	NOV	DEC
Product knowledge												
Pre-planning												
Objectives												
Introduction												
Participation												
Handling objections												
Use of benefits												
Visual aids												
Third-party proof												
Investment merit												
Closing techniques												
Merchandising												
Range selling												
TOTAL												

Organization	JAN	FEB	MAR	APR	MAY	JUN	JUL	AUG	SEP	OCT	NOV	DEC
Territory planning												
Use of time												
Reporting												
Records												
Sales statistics												
New account												
Follow-up												
Care of equipment												
TOTAL												

Attributes	JAN	FEB	MAR	APR	MAY	JUN	JUL	AUG	SEP	OCT	NOV	DEC
Enthusiasm and drive												
Training and self-development												
Appearance												
Punctuality												
Cooperation												
Customer relations												
TOTAL												
GRAND TOTAL												

to recognize the difference between removing a demotivating factor and accentuating a motivating one. Removing a demotivating factor will not of itself bring about motivation. All it will do is to stop the moaning and groaning about the situation. In contrast to this, accentuating or adding to the motivating factors will undoubtedly lead to a higher commitment to the work.

Worksheet 2 enables you to establish exactly what these factors will be for your organization.

WORKSHEET 2   Motivational climate

Get your salespeople to consider the various things, incidents or situations, that have happened to them in their work over the last, say 6 months.(You can select the time period). Then ask them to make brief notes under the headings shown on the form.

Those things I found *DISSATISFYING*	*Those things which gave me* *SATISFACTION*

Find ways to reduce or eliminate as many of these factors as possible.

Find ways to build on or add to these factors. These are the real *motivators*.

9 The pricing plan

Reasons for a pricing plan

Pricing is a key part of the marketing mix and needs to be managed intelligently, in the same way as the other parts. Generally, pricing is included as part of product/segment plans and doesn't appear as a separate entity. This can disguise some of the complex issues to be found in pricing.

Cost-plus pricing

Traditionally, pricing has been the remit of accountants. Their concern was mainly about the impact of price on margin and hence revenue. The weaknesses of this approach are:

1 Product can be overpriced because of arbitrary loading of production and other overheads.
2 There is no room for strategic thinking.
3 Products can be eliminated from the range, regardless of their synergy with others.

In contrast, marketers look at price in terms of its influence on demand.

Competitive pricing

The possible pricing spectrum is:

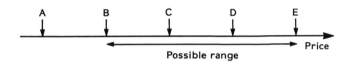

A = marginal cost per unit
B = lowest price limit in the market
C = average cost per unit

D = 'going rate' price in the market
E = top end price limit in the market

Try Exercise 9.1

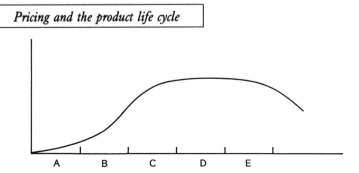

Pricing and the product life cycle

A   B   C   D   E

Different positions of the life cycle call for different pricing strategies.
A   Introduction
Either

1   Price low to win high market share.
2   Price high in recognition of novelty and prestige.

B   Growth
Price competitively to win market share.

C   Maturity
As per the growth phase.

D   Saturation
Stabilize price; consider raising it.

E   Decline
Raise price

Try Exercise 9.2

Product positioning

Pricing can influence the position of a product in the market, e.g. a high price can convey an image of better quality, design or exclusiveness. Here is one example of product positioning.

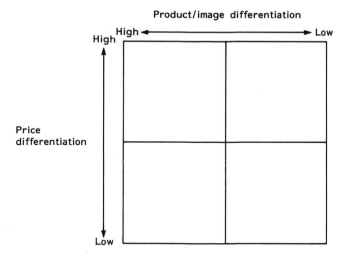

Better positioning beats the competition.

Channel discounts

If there are intermediaries, they have to be rewarded in return for their services, i.e. there has to be a total channel margin allowed for in 'price to customer' calculations. Discounts against nominal price lists can be in the form of:

1 Trade discounts.
2 Quantity discounts.
3 Promotional discounts.
4 Cash discounts.

How the total margin is sliced for distributors is a matter of 'trade-offs' of costs versus the added value of using distributors.

Try Exercise 9.3

Factors affecting price

Price can be influenced by:

● Marketing objectives.
● The cost structure.

- Legal constraints.
- Consumer attitudes.
- Competition (direct).
- Competition (substitutes).
- Company/product image.
- Economic situation.

Try Exercises 9.4 and 9.5

Questions raised for the company

1 Q: Is it possible to develop a sound pricing policy if one's costing is suspect?

   A: While 'prices' and 'costs' are separate entities, it is essential that a company has an accurate costing system. Without this there is no point of reference to put pricing into perspective.

2 Q: What is the true price of a product?

   A: Seen by the buyer it is purchase price and cost of introduction; this can include training costs, maintenance, energy consumption, disruption costs, consumables, floor space, etc. However, these items can be a source of differential advantage over competing products, which in effect provides a 'better price' in real money terms.

3 Q: Is it better to price high or low?

   A: It depends on a number of factors, such as market share and so on. It is as well to remember, however, that if you try to have the lowest price, someone will usually try to go even lower. This is a difficult battle to win.

Introduction

Clearly, pricing is a marketing 'tool' just as much as advertising, promotions and the use of the salesforce. Moreover, it is generally easier and quicker to change a price than it is to alter an advertising campaign, revamp a sales promotion, or to deploy the salesforce in a different manner.

Pricing decisions not only affect the revenue the company can earn, but also they influence demand, thereby making an impact on the quantities sold. Yet for all this, few companies have a pricing plan. Indeed, rather than a positive strategy, the very topic often becomes a battleground in a war of apparently conflicting interests between marketers and accountants.

Exercise 9.1 looks at how to set a competitive price for a product or service, taking into account a number of different factors which can have a bearing on the pricing decision.

Exercise 9.2 is concerned with selecting the price.

Exercise 9.3 provides some insights into the real impact of price discounts.

Exercise 9.4 is a self-scoring questionnaire which gives you some assessment about your readiness to get involved in aggressive pricing situations.

Exercise 9.5 poses a number of awkward questions about pricing and gives you an opportunity of testing out your expertise.

Exercise 9.1 Competitive pricing

This exercise will enable you to use pricing in a creative way, one which will support your marketing plan. It will use information from your marketing audit and a few new pieces of data to help you to arrive at a sensible Pricing Plan for your products or services.

It goes without saying that unless the company has an accurate costing system, one that realistically reflects its internal situation, then it will be impossible to establish anything like a sensible pricing policy. The reason for this will become self-evident as you provide the information requested below.

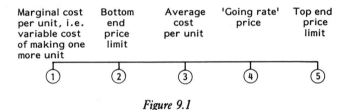

Figure 9.1

Figure 9.1 shows some key positions on the costing/pricing continuum.

Taking just *one* of your company's major products or services, enter on the worksheet the actual figures that correspond to the numbers 1 to 5, in the positions marked in Figure 9.1, i.e. the actual marginal cost, bottom end price limit, etc.

When considering the average cost please remember that costing systems that allocate fixed costs to all products in the range, while being popular, can produce some very misleading results, especially if the basis of cost allocation is somewhat arbitrary. Some products can never survive the cost load they have to carry. Knowing what the customer is prepared to pay for your chosen product/service (the going rate price), consider different costing options, with the objective of getting the average cost per unit as low as possible, thereby providing you with a wider range of pricing options.

Consider other products and services and repeat this process for them Worksheet 1 is useful in order to establish the range of discretion open to you, but the more important task will be to identify where exactly on this scale to select your price position.

WORKSHEET   Cost price continuum (Ex. 9.1)

PRODUCT/SERVICE	1 Marginal cost per unit	2 Bottom end price limit per unit	3 Av. cost per unit	4 Going rate price per unit	5 Top end price limit per unit
Example	£6.50	£8.50	£10	£13	£20

Exercise 9.2   Selecting the price

It can be shown that there are a number of factors that can influence your ultimate choice of price. These will be considered in turn.

CORPORATE OBJECTIVES

If the corporate objectives dictate that it will be important to generate short-term profits for your chosen product/service, it would be reasonable to select a high price, somewhere between 4 and 5 on the scale established in Figure 9.1. Alternatively, if the aim is to extend market share, then a position between 3 and 4 would be more suitable.

You can see from this example that whatever the nature of the corporate or marketing objectives for your chosen product or service, it is possible to select a position somewhere on the scale which appears to be most appropriate. Now you select a position for your chosen product and record the price on the worksheet where indicated.

PORTFOLIO MATRIX

It has been shown that a different marketing strategy would be required according to which quadrant 'housed' your chosen product. Generally speaking, this would mean that prices should be selected as follows:

(a) *'Question mark'*. Price competitively to get market share.
(b) *'Star'*. Price to maintain/increase market share.
(c) *'Cash cow'*. Stabilize or even raise price.
(d) *'Dog'*. Raise price.

With these guidelines in mind, select a position on the 1–5 scale for your product/service and again record the price on the worksheet.

LIFE CYCLE

Your chosen product's position on its life cycle will also be significant when calculating its price:

(*a*) Introduction stage. Either price low to capture market share, or if there is genuine novelty or innovation associated with the product, price high in recognition of its prestige value.
(*b*) Growth stage. Price low to get market share.
(*c*) Maturity. As for growth stage.
(*d*) Saturation. Stabilize price, consider raising it.
(*e*) Decline. Raise price.

Using these suggestions, select a position for your chosen product on the 1–5 scale and, again, note the price on Worksheet 2.

PRODUCT POSITION

Your price will have to take into account the marketing profile you are trying to establish for your chosen product. If yours is the biggest, the best, the most technologically advanced product, then your price ought to echo the fact. Similarly, if your target is just high-income customers, your price should reflect that exclusivity. The converse will be true for down-market economy models, where a lower price would be more consistent with the product position.

Carefully consider your product position and use your judgement to 'score' a position on the 1–5 scale. Record your choice of price on the worksheet.

CURRENT COMPETITION

Analyse the prices charged by your competitors for their versions of your product or service. Will these influence your ultimate choice of price?

Where does this information suggest you position the price on the 1–5 scale? Enter your answer on the worksheet.

POTENTIAL COMPETITION

Another consideration you will have to take into account will be the extent to which your chosen price might either attract or repel competitors. Clearly, if you can get away with charging high prices and making correspondingly high margins, then it will not be long before others become interested in your sphere of business.

Estimate the price you can charge using the 1–5 scale as a reference. Note the selected price on Worksheet 2.

CHANNELS OF DISTRIBUTION

If your business is one where you need to use intermediaries to reach your customers, then, in return for their services, they will expect a reward in the shape of a 'mark-up' or margin on the goods. Thus the price you charge at the factory gate has to be profitable for you, yet still allow the intermediary a fair margin without leading to an excessively high price for the ultimate consumer. What will this mean for your pricing decision?

Choose a position on the 1–5 scale and enter the price on the worksheet.

DIFFERENTIAL BENEFITS

If your product or service provides differential customer benefits which your competitors do not provide, then you could justify a higher price and gain the reward from higher revenue.

Your option for doing this might be limited by some of the other considerations above. For example, it might be better to use your product advantage to gain a larger market share. Nevertheless, if the benefit analysis you carried out in Chapter 4 suggests any room for manoeuvre on pricing, score the new choice on the 1–5 scale and enter the actual figure on the worksheet.

CONSUMER ATTITUDES

Consumer attitudes to your particular product/service or to your company, because of its name and reputation, might also influence your ultimate choice of price. To what extent will this be the case? Again select a price position on the 1–5 scale that you believe can be justified as a result of consumer attitudes to your product.

Record the price on the worksheet.

You have now looked at nine different factors that are known to influence pricing. These have been considered in isolation and a notional price position for your product has been calculated against each factor.

The price positions were established by using a cost/price continuum, with key positions numbered 1–5. The actual money value of each of these positions was calculated in the worksheet of Exercise 9.1.

The worksheet in this exercise is a record of the results you have attributed to the various pricing factors. You will now use this information in the following way:

1   Find the average price position for your product by adding up the

column of prices and dividing it by the number of factors you used (an example is shown on the worksheet). This average figure would seem to be the 'best fit' when taking all the factors into account, and should therefore be selected as the price for your chosen product, unless, of course, there are other factors known to you which would militate against this decision.

2   Now repeat this process for other products or services.

WORKSHEET   Factors affecting price (Ex. 9.2)

		Example (based on example on preceding Worksheet)	Prod. 1	Prod. 2	Prod. 3	Prod. 4
1	Corporate objectives	£18.00				
2	Portfolio matrix	£16.00				
3	Life cycle analysis	£16.00				
4	Product position	£10.00				
5	Current competition	£12.00				
6	Potential competition	£10.00				
7	Channels of dist.	not applic.				
8	Differential benefits	£9.00				
9	Consumer attitudes	£9.00				
	Total score	£100.00				
	Number of factors	8				
	Suggested price average	£12.50				

CRITIQUE OF EXAMPLE PROVIDED ON WORKSHEETS

This approach to pricing raises many important issues. In the example provided it is quite evident that the corporate objectives are for the product to generate revenue. The positions on the portfolio matrix and life cycle also appear to support this strategy of pricing high.

But look at some of the other factors. The product position would not appear to justify a high price, there seems to be few differential benefits and consumer attitudes are not very positive. In addition it looks as if the company will have to price below the 'going rate' if it is going to cope with the competition.

Result – a compromise price of £12.50p unit.

Moral – if the company wants to price high, it must upgrade the product in terms of providing more differential benefits and work to improve customer attitudes.

Alternatively, or in addition, it should carefully re-examine the actual costs and its costing system and by doing so try to improve the margin that would be achievable at £12.50p. By these means, it might well obtain results similar to its original objectives of pricing high.

Personal notes

Exercise 9.3 The use of discounts

To give a price reduction, which is really what a discount is, appears on the surface to be a fairly straightforward and easy-to-apply mechanism for stimulating demand. However, it is not always fully appreciated how many extra products have to be sold merely to break even, i.e. to get back to the original situation.

Here is a simple example. Suppose a company had sales of 100 units of a product per week, priced at £10. Thus the total income was £1,000 and this yielded a profit of £200. The marketing director of the company decides that a 10 per cent reduction in price will stimulate a demand in sales. What new level of sales in units would have to be achieved to break even?

Write your answer here ....

Probably this was how you calculated your figure:

	Units	Price	Total income	Profit
Original situation	100	£10	£1,000	£200

Since 100 units yielded £200 profit, profit per unit = £2. With price reduced to £9 (10 per cent reduction) new profit per unit = £1.

	Units	Price	Total income	Profit
Therefore new situation becomes	200	£9	£1,800	£200

Thus the company would have to double its sale of units to maintain its existing profit level if it sold at the new lower price. Perhaps some questions would have to be asked about the feasibility of this happening.

To avoid having to make tedious calculations each time you contemplate making a price reduction, Table 9.1 provides an easy-to-use reference.

Table 9.1   **Effects of price reductions**

	5%	10%	15%	20%	25%	30%	35%	40%
			And your present gross profit is					

If you cut your price	You need to sell this much more to break even							
	%	%	%	%	%	%	%	%
1%	25.0	11.1	7.1	5.3	4.2	3.4	2.9	2.6
2%	66.6	25.0	15.4	11.1	8.7	7.1	6.1	5.3
3%	150.0	42.0	25.0	17.6	13.6	11.1	9.4	8.1
4%	400.0	66.6	36.4	25.0	19.0	15.4	12.9	11.1
5%	–	100.0	50.0	33.3	25.0	20.0	16.7	14.3
6%	–	150.0	66.7	42.9	31.6	25.0	20.7	17.6
7%	–	233.3	87.5	53.8	38.9	30.4	25.0	21.2
8%	–	400.0	114.3	66.7	47.1	36.4	29.6	25.0
9%	–	1,000.0	150.0	81.8	56.3	42.9	34.6	29.0
10%	–	–	200.0	100.0	66.7	50.0	40.0	33.3
11%	–	–	275.0	122.2	78.6	57.9	45.8	37.9
12%	–	–	400.0	150.0	92.3	66.7	52.2	42.9
13%	–	–	650.0	185.7	108.3	76.5	59.1	48.1
14%	–	–	1,400.0	233.3	127.3	87.5	66.7	53.8
15%	–	–	–	300.0	150.0	100.0	76.8	60.0
16%	–	–	–	400.0	177.8	1,144.3	84.2	66.7
17%	–	–	–	566.7	212.5	100.8	94.4	73.9
18%	–	–	–	900.0	257.1	150.0	105.9	81.8
19%	–	–	–	1,900.0	316.7	172.7	118.8	90.5
20%	–	–	–	–	400.0	200.0	133.3	100.0
21%	–	–	–	–	525.0	233.3	150.0	110.5
22%	–	–	–	–	733.3	275.0	169.2	122.2
23%	–	–	–	–	1,115.0	328.6	191.7	135.3
24%	–	–	–	–	2,400.0	400.0	218.2	150.0
25%	–	–	–	–	–	500.0	250.0	166.7

Example: Your present gross margin is 25 per cent and you cut your selling price by 10 per cent. Locate 10 per cent in the left-hand column. Now follow across to the column headed 25 per cent. You find you will need to sell 66.7 per cent *more* units.

Note. Exercises 9.4 and 9.5 are based on John Winkler's work on pricing and I am indebted to him for the ideas. Readers are recommended to follow this up by reading *Pricing for Results* (Butterworth-Heinemann 1985).

Exercise 9.4   Questionnaire

This exercise is really designed for personal insight, but you won't fail to notice that you could use it equally well to analyse your marketing director or chief executive.

Consider these statements and *quickly* tick the score which most aptly represents your position.

		Very true of me	Usually true of me	No feeling either way	Usually untrue of me	Very untrue of me
1	If a rival company is cheaper, I want to match or beat its price.	5	4	3	2	1
2	I would like to talk to competitors about equalizing prices.	1	2	3	4	5
3	I'm prepared to start a discount battle any time; I believe the first one in wins.	5	4	3	2	1
4	Before quoting a special price I will always ask 'Why?'	1	2	3	4	5
5	I'm prepared to lose some deals on price.	1	2	3	4	5
6	I always try to keep it simple if I can! '10 per cent off' is the way to do it.	5	4	3	2	1
7	I try not to publish discounts. I perfer to negotiate them individually.	1	2	3	4	5
8	I am always prepared to offer bigger discounts than I allow those working for me to offer.	5	4	3	2	1
9	I believe that most people will jump at a 10 per cent discount.	5	4	3	2	1
10	I believe that people who start savage price wars often live to regret it.	1	2	3	4	5

Now add up the total score for all your ticks and write it in the box on the right.

SCORING AND INTERPRETATION OF EXERCISE 9.4

The questions are not very subtle and so very good scores are required from this exercise. The lowest score for each question is the best, but an extremely low score, *of 12 or less*, might show you to be rather inflexible. You might well be used to working in an industry where the quality content of what you offer is very high, with prices that reflect this. In these circumstances you would tend to avoid price fights as much as you can.

A score of 13–16 is a good score – you will hold on and make sensible, profitable deals most of the time. Although you might lose out here and there on high volume, you would rather make the largest profits than the largest sales.

Above 25 – you are a potential warmonger, probably used to working at the bottom end of some very tough markets, with some rapacious buyers. There's one other thing, and you might not like to hear this. These buyers are probably taking you to the cleaners.

Exercise 9.5   Awkward questions on pricing

Here are some hypothetical questions concerning pricing. How would you deal with these situations?

Question 1

You are the Marketing Director of a pharmaceuticals company in a country where there is no equivalent of a National Health Service, and patients have to pay for the drugs they use. Your company produces a life-support drug. Once patients have been treated with it, they must stay on it continuously to survive. This drug has been outdated by a machine which treats new patients and, as a result, your market is gradually eroding.

Should you adopt:

(*a*) A system based on cost-plus.
(*b*) A system based on what the market will bear.
(*c*) A system based on some notion of morality.
(*d*) A system based on what the competition charges.

Question 2

You have an excess of stock of a poor line to clear. You must shift this stock in order to raise money to invest in better products. What is your view of promotional pricing? Do you:

(*a*) Actively encourage it all the time?
(*b*) Offer it only to your best customers?
(*c*) Refuse to use it at all?
(*d*) Use it sparingly, outside normal markets?
(*e*) Use it a little, but create an impression that you use it a lot, through advertising etc.?

Question 3

You want to price aggressively in order to take over a major part of a total market. What level of price discount should you offer in a normal consumer product market, as a minimum, to make the market turn to you in a meaningful way?

(*a*) 10 per cent off competitors' prices.
(*b*) 15 per cent off competitors' prices.

(c) 20 per cent off competitors' prices.
(d) 30 per cent off competitors' prices.
(e) Between 40 and 50 per cent off competitors' prices.

Question 4
If you average out all the prices of consumer products in a given market, you can arrive at an average price. Yours is the biggest selling brand in this market. Together with your two nearest competitors you share 60 per cent of the market. Measured against the average market price, where would you expect your brand leader product to be positioned?

(a) 10 per cent less than the average price.
(b) On, or closely around, the average price.
(c) 20 per cent less than the average price.
(d) 7 per cent above the average price.

ANSWERS TO EXERCISE 9.5

Question 1

(a) Score +1.
(b) Score −5. They will pay anything to stay alive, but how can you live with yourself?
(c) Score +5.
(d) Score +1.

Question 2

(a) Score 0.
(b) Score +1. A poor tactic because it will make your best customers look for bargains all the time. It might generate some goodwill.
(c) Score +1. Too rigid.
(d) Score +5. Get rid of it altogether if you can, otherwise go for (e).
(e) Score +4. A technique used by some supermarkets. A few loss leaders in reality, but all of them promoted very heavily. But you will still be attracting price cutting in your market, and you will have to advertise your price cuts as well as give the discounts away. This can be expensive unless the volume sales justify it.

Question 3

(a) Score 0.
(b) Score +1.

(*c*) Score +2.
(*d*) Score +3.
(*e*) Score +4.

Question 4

(*a*) Score 0.
(*b*) Score +2.
(*c*) Score −2.
(*d*) Score +5.

INTERPRETATION OF SCORES

15 or more. You did very well and/or are very experienced.
10–14. Think a bit harder before making decisions.
Less than 10. Don't engage in pricing decision-making.

10 The distribution plan

> *Physical distribution*

This chapter obviously applies only to tangible products.

Physical distribution ensures products get to the right place, on time, and in the right condition. In some businesses, distribution costs can amount to 20 per cent of the selling price. There are five components to manage:

1 *Facilities*. The number, size and geographical location of storage and distribution depots.
2 *Inventory*. The stockholding levels throughout the distribution chain consistent with customers' service expectations.
3 *Transport*. Made up of transport, delivery, schedules etc.
4 *Communications*. There is also a flow of information, for example, order processing, invoicing, forecasting, etc.
5 *Unitization*. The way in which goods are packaged and assembled into large units, e.g. palletization, container loads, etc.
   Considerable savings can be made by innovating in this area.

> *Channels for reaching customers*

There is a range of possible distribution channels e.g.

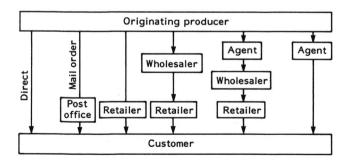

Which one is best for competitive advantage?

Try Exercises 10.1 and 10.2

Availability and customer service package

Customer expectations about product availability will vary from market to market. In theory, 100 per cent availability should be the norm. In practice, a compromise might have to be found, say 95 per cent, because the additional cost of providing that extra 5 per cent can be prohibitive. In addition, often such high levels of customer service are not necessary. Balance the benefits to the customer with cost to you.

Factors which impact on customer service

These include:

- Frequency of delivery.
- Time from order to delivery.
- Emergency deliveries when required.
- Accuracy of paperwork.
- Stock availability.
- Reliability of deliveries etc.

Key factors should be identified and researched with a view to improving them.

Try Exercises 10.3 and 10.4

Distribution planning

The approach should follow these steps:

1 Determine marketing objectives.
2 Evaluate changing conditions in distribution at all levels.
3 Determine the distribution task within marketing strategy.
4 Establish a policy in terms of type, number and level of outlets to be used.
5 Set performance standards for distributors.
6 Obtain performance information.
7 Compare actual with anticipated performance.
8 Make improvements where necessary.

Try Exercise 10.5

Questions raised for the company

1 Q: How important is it to have a distribution plan?

   A: It depends on the type of business. In some industries distribution costs amount to 20 per cent or more of sales revenue. Distribution is the Cinderella of marketing, but can often be the area where a competitive edge can be won – through planning.

2 Q: Can services be distributed? After all, they can't be stocked.

   A: No, but services can be franchised. Once a rational decision has been made to use channels, it is the company's responsibility to work at developing a good business relationship based on trust and mutual respect. It is to both parties' mutual advantage.

4 Q: Are there any new developments in distribution?

   A: Franchising is becoming popular. In addition, some transport contractors now also supply warehousing, inventory control and other services, in effect providing the manufacturer with an 'off-the-shelf' distribution facility.

Introduction

For many businesses, distribution plays a small part in their marketing plans. When it is considered, the prime concern seems to focus on the physical aspects, the logistics of getting goods transported from the company to the customer.

Distribution, however, embraces a much broader concept than just the delivery of goods. In addition, it takes into account the strategic importance of distribution channels and the potential value of channel intermediaries. It also ensures that 'customer service' is kept in the forefront of the company's deliberations about its marketing policies. The exercises in this section mirror this broad view of distribution.

Exercise 10.1 helps you to decide whether or not intermediaries are required in your type of business.

Exercise 10.2 explains how intermediaries might be selected.

Exercise 10.3 is designed solely to get you to think about your own customer service from the customer's point of view.

Exercise 10.4 looks at the total customer service package and will enable you to check how yours compares with those of your competitors, and, equally importantly, what steps you will have to take to improve your competitiveness.

Exercise 10.5 addresses the physical aspects of distribution.

Exercise 10.6 invites you to use all the information generated in Exercises 10.1 to 10.5 and integrate it into a distribution plan.

Exercise 10.1   Do we need channel intermediaries?

At first sight, the choice of distribution channel is deceptively easy. After all, basically there are only three options from which to choose:

1   To sell direct to the customer/user.
2   To sell to customers/users through intermediaries.
3   To use a combination of 1 and 2, i.e. dual distribution.

The final choice will always be something of a compromise, with, on the one hand, the desire to keep control of the distribution of one's products or services, and, on the other hand, the practical need to keep distribution costs to a bearable level.

the worksheet is designed to help you to make a choice about channels of distribution. This is what you do:

1   Take each product/service in your portfolio in turn and subject them to the algorithm given on the worksheet.
2   Note the decision for each product, i.e. sell direct or use channel intermediaries. Do these seem the best decisions or can you see good reasons for ignoring them?
3   In working through the algorithm, can you see a case for dual distribution for some products or services? For example, do you sell direct to some customers or regions and sell through intermediaries to others. Remember the major problem associated with dual distribution is determining a fair division of the market between yourself (as the supplier) and the intermediary(ies).

Use the space below to record the decisions from using the worksheet or to make any other relevant notes.

Notes

WORKSHEET   Distribution channel algorithm (Ex. 10.1)

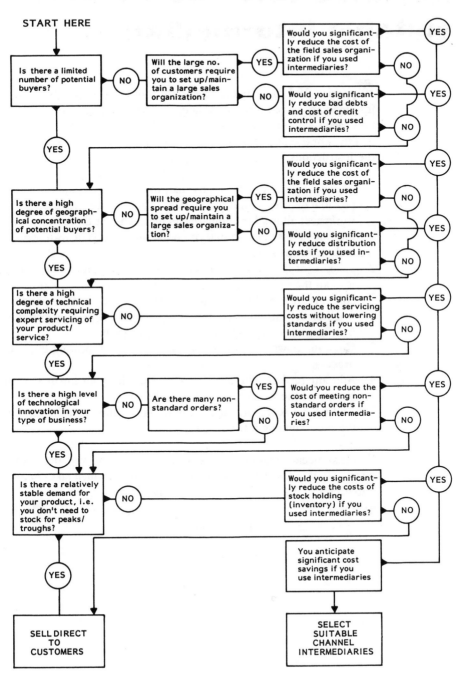

Exercise 10.2 Selecting a suitable intermediary

Exercise 10.1 helped to answer the question of whether or not an intermediary is required. Assuming the answer is affirmative, you are now faced with selecting a suitable candidate to play that role.

The worksheet should help you in your decision-making. Here are the instructions for using it:

1 Make a note of organizations that, on the surface, appear to be possible choices as intermediaries. (You will see that the worksheet allows for comparisons between just three prospective intermediaries. You should of course draw up your own form to include as many as you like.)

2 Looking at the list of evaluation criteria, take criterion 1 and apply it to all the prospective channel intermediaries. Place scores in columns A, B and C – a number between 0 and 10, depending on whether the intermediary is a very poor fit against this criterion (zero score) or an extremely good fit (10 points).

3 Continue down the list of evaluation criteria, repeating this scoring process.

4 Add any further criteria that are relevant for your business to the bottom of the list and score them likewise.

5 Add up the scores in each column. The highest total represents the most suitable intermediary.

You may decide that some criteria are more important than others on this list. In this case use a points weighting system which takes importance into account. An example of a weighting system is given in Exercise 4.2 (p. 45).

WORKSHEET   Criteria for selecting intermediaries (Ex. 10.2)

Evaluation criteria	Prospective intermediaries		
	A	B	C
1 Currently deals with our target market segment			
2 Is prepared to deal with target market segment			
3 Salesforce is sufficiently large			
4 Salesforce is well trained			
5 Regional locations well positioned			
6 Promotional policies consistent with ours			
7 Budgets are adequate			
8 Can provide customer after sales service			
9 Product policies consistent with ours			
10 Does not carry competitor lines			
11 Prepared to carry adequate stocks			
12 Prepared to carry range/cover			
13 Suitable storage facilities			
14 Is creditworthy			
15 Management attitudes compatible with ours			
16 Has suitable reputation			
(Add others that are relevant)			
17			
18			
19			
20			
21			
22			
23			
24			
25			
26			
27			
28			
29			
30			
TOTAL			

Exercise 10.3 Customer service audit*

Before getting into more detail about customer service, start by completing this customer service audit. If you have 'No' in more than three questions, or if you have difficulty answering the open-ended questions, you may have a serious customer service problem in your organization.

1 Do you have a written customer service policy?

Yes ....

No ....

2 Is this given a wide circulation within the company?

Yes ....

No ....

3 Do customers receive a copy of this policy?

Yes ....

No ....

4 What are the three most crucial aspects of customer service as they impinge upon your marketing effectiveness?

1 ....

2 ....

3 ....

5 Is any attempt made to monitor your customer service performance on these three dimensions?

* This audit is based on an audit constructed by Professor Martin Christopher, a colleague at Cranfield School of Management, and is used with his kind permission.

Yes ....

No ....

6 Do you monitor competitive customer service offerings?

Yes ....

No ....

7 Do you believe that within your company there is adequate knowledge of the true costs of providing customer service?

Yes ....

No ....

8 Which function(s) has responsibility for customer service management?

....

....

9 Where does customer service management fit in relation to the marketing function? (Draw an organizational chart if necessary).

10 Do you have an established method of communications for your customers to contact you about some aspect of their order after the order has been entered?

Yes ....

No ....

11   Do you have (*a*) a single point of contact for customers or (*b*) do certain departments handle different types of inquiries/complaints?

Yes (*a*)   (*b*)

No (*a*)   (*b*)

12   What do you think are the major areas of weakness in your current approach to customer service management?

....

....

....

....

....

Exercise 10.4   The customer service package

Customer service has been defined as the percentage of occasions the product or service is available to the customer *when* and *where* he or she wants it. Obviously, to operate service levels at 100% might, and often does, impose a crippling cost on the supplier, yet to drop below an acceptable level is to surrender one's market share to a competitor.

Research has shown that to improve one's service level by even a small amount when it is already at a high level can become expensive (the law of diminishing returns). Therefore the marketer will have to be certain about the actual levels of customer service provided and to have a greater understanding of customer expectations and needs. It will be highly likely that different market segments will require different levels of customer service.

The ultimate choice of service level for a specific product will be tempered by other influential factors:

1   The contribution to fixed costs, e.g. can it bear the cost of an upgraded service level?
2   The nature of the market, e.g. are there substitute products?
3   The nature of the competition, e.g. do they offer better service levels?
4   The nature of the distribution channel, e.g. do we sell direct or through intermediaries?

The key to marketing success is for your company to develop a customer service package – one that embraces product availability, with attractive order cycle times, and mechanisms for minimizing customer inconvenience arising from order cycle variations.

The worksheet is designed to help you to arrive at a more competitive customer service package or, if this is too expensive, to devise an alternative. The instructions are provided on the worksheet. The space below is for any notes you might wish to make about these issues.

Personal notes

WORKSHEET Developing a customer service package (Ex. 10.4)

Take one of your market segments and decide what would make the best 'package' by putting a tick against the appropriate items in column 1, i.e. what does your marketing strategy suggest?

In column 2 tick the items that go to make the best competitor package.
In column 3 estimate if the provision of your item is *Better, Equal* or *Worse* than the best competitor.
In column 4 indicate the relative cost of improving where you compete unfavourably with the best competitor, i.e. *High, Medium* or *Low*.
In column 5 list improvement actions to upgrade the service package to match the best competitor.
In column 6 consider alternative packages, i.e. to fight on different grounds.

Repeat this process for all other market segments.

Components of customer service	(1) Market strategy suggestions	(2) Best competitor	(3) Better Equal Worse	(4) Comp. cost H, M, L	(5) Actions to upgrade cust. serv.	(6) Alt. package
Frequency of delivery						
Time from order to delivery						
Reliability of delivery						
Emergency deliveries when required						
Stock availability						
Continuity of supply						
Advice on non-availability						
Convenience of placing orders						
Acknowledgement of orders						
Accuracy of invoices						
Quality of sales representation						
Regularity of calls by sales reps.						
Monitoring of stock levels						
Credit terms offered						
Handling of customer queries						
Quality of outer packaging						
Well-stacked pallets						
Easy to read use by dates on outers						
Clear handling instructions on outers						
Quality of inner package for handling						

Worksheet (cont.)

Components of customer service	(1) Market strategy suggest- ions	(2) Best compet- itor	(3) Better Equal Worse	(4) Comp. cost H,M,L	(5) Actions to upgrade cust. serv.	(6) Alt. package
Quality of inner package for display						
Consultation on new developments, e.g. products or packaging						
Regular review of product range coordination between production, distribution and marketing						
Add others which are relevant for your business						
....						
....						
....						
....						
....						
....						
....						

Personal notes

Exercise 10.5 Physical distribution

It has been shown that there are five areas to be considered when it comes to physical distribution, the so-called 'distribution mix'. They are: facilities, inventory, transport, communications, and unitization.

FACILITIES

Having established the level of customer service required by each market segment, you must reappraise the location of your own plants and warehouses in order to ensure they are situated in geographically suitable positions *vis à vis* the customers. If the nature of demand and the location of major customers is forecast to change dramatically, then re-locating manufacturing units and/or warehouses is an option that, in the long term, can lead to savings due to reduced distribution costs.

Such decisions cannot be taken lightly. For most organizations their facilities are taken as fixed, certainly in the short term.

INVENTORY

The holding of stock, whether by design or accident, is always a costly business. Therefore it is important to know the comparative costs of holding stocks of different products in order to arrive at a sensible stockholding policy.

Worksheet 1 enables you to calculate the various components of inventory cost for each of your major products and thereby produce the necessary cost data. Once in possession of this information, it might become necessary for you to revise the customer service package or indeed earlier deliberations about channel intermediaries.

TRANSPORT

This is the area that many people are familiar with, and, as such, has traditionally received most management attention. Worksheet 2 shows a typical way of calculating the merits or demerits of various forms of transporting goods to customers. Try it, using some of your own products as study vehicles.

While cost is an important determinant in the choice of transport, frequency of service and reliability are often just as important. Regular monitoring of transport costs is to be recommended if distribution costs are to be held in check.

COMMUNICATIONS

It is often overlooked that accompanying the flow of materials through the distribution channel there is also a flow of information in the form of orders, invoices, demand forecasts, delivery schedules, etc. Each of these 'communications' is likely to be an integral part of your customer service package, and yet, in all probability, they were set up for your own company's administrative convenience.

Look at all your communications associated with distribution and put yourself in the customer's shoes. For example, how sensible does your ordering system seem when viewed from the other end? Get out and speak to some actual customers and seek their views. Anything that can be done to simplify or speed-up communications must be to your company's benefit – and it doesn't have to cost you money to improve the situation.

UNITIZATION

Assess whether or not it is possible to make your products more acceptable to users or intermediaries, e.g. for handling or stacking, by packaging them into different sized units such as shrink-wrapped bulk packs, pallet loads, container loads, etc. It is often possible to win substantial cost savings in terms of handling or warehousing by considering this aspect of distribution.

WORKSHEET 1 Comparative inventory costs (Ex. 10.5)

Area of cost	Product (1)	(2)	(3)	(4)	(5)
Warehouse costs (rent, rates, heat, light, etc.)					
Labour costs					
Losses/shrinkage					
Deterioration/damage					
Insurance					
Interest (on funds tied up in stock)					
Administrative costs					
Other costs relevant to your specific business					
. . . .					
. . . .					
. . . .					
. . . .					
. . . .					
. . . .					
. . . .					
. . . .					
. . . .					
. . . .					
. . . .					
. . . .					
. . . .					
. . . .					
. . . .					
. . . .					
. . . .					
. . . .					
. . . .					
. . . .					
. . . .					
. . . .					

For the purpose of this worksheet take the cost per item, or unit; or you can, if you prefer, just express the costs as a percentage of the book value of the stock.

WORKSHEET 2   Comparative physical distribution costs (Ex. 10.5)

Method of physical distribution	Product/service				
	(1)	(2)	(3)	(4)	(5)
Use own transport Contract hire Use carriers Other forms of road transport					
Passenger rail train Freight train Red Star Parcel Other forms of rail transport					
Boat on deck Boat in hold Hovercraft Other forms of sea transport					
Air parcel Air freight Other forms of air transport					
1st class post 2nd class post Parcel post Other postal methods					
Other transport methods					

Use either cost per item or unit, or you can, if you prefer, express the costs as a percentage of the book value of your stock.

Exercise 10.6   The distribution plan

From the foregoing study material you will by now have highlighted several ways of improving distribution in your company or have confirmed that existing practices were well chosen. In order that your effort is not wasted, it will be important to encapsulate your major findings in the distribution plan. Here is a suggestion for how this can be done:

1   Show how, in the light of the company's marketing objectives and strategy, the distribution task needs to be defined.
2   From your work, show where current practice supports this definition of the distribution task and where it does not.
3   Using the data you have assembled, recommend:

   (a) A distribution policy in terms of type, number and level of outlet to be used.
   (b) Performance standards for the distribution organization.
   (c) Where changes in the distribution organization are required.
   (d) Ways of monitoring performance as the plan unfolds.

Personal notes

11 Marketing information, forecasting and organizing for marketing planning

Marketing information

Marketing information is at the heart of the company's ability to plan. *Marketing research* is concerned with research into the whole marketing process (*market research* is research about markets).

Try Exercise 11.1

Types of marketing research

1 Internal – analysis of sales records, advertising levels, price v volume, etc.
2 External – to complement internal research.
3 Reactive – people respond to questionnaires, structured interviews, etc.
4 Non-reactive – interpretation of observed phenomena, e.g. filming customers in a store, listening to customer panels, etc.

There are pros and cons for each type; therefore, a mix can be useful.

Try Exercise 11.2

How much to spend
Can be based on the theory of probability and expected value. For example, a product costs £100k to develop. There is an estimated 10 per cent chance of failure. The maximum cost therefore = £100k × 0.1 = £10k. Therefore it is worth spending this amount to prevent the loss.

Marketing information system (MIS)
A system to facilitate information flows needs to be developed so that there are appropriate inputs and that correct data get to the users in a sensible form.

Forecasting

Forecasting can be of two types:

1 *Macro* – forecasting markets in total.
2 *Micro* – detailed unit forecasts.

Which to choose depends upon the:

(*a*) accuracy required,
(*b*) availability of data,
(*c*) time horizon,
(*d*) position of the product in its life cycle (macro at early stage).

Techniques for forecasting:
Quantitative – based on facts.
Qualitative – based on experience and judgement.

Try Exercise 11.3

Organizational barriers

A number of potential barriers exist:

1 *Cognitive* – not knowing enough about marketing planning.
2 *Cultural* – the company culture is not sufficiently developed for marketing planning.
3 *Political* – the culture carriers feel threatened by marketing.
4 *Resources* – not enough resources are allocated to marketing.
5 *Structural* – lack of a plan and organization for planning.
6 *Lack of an MIS.*

Centralization v decentralization

For multi-unit/international organizations there are two possibilities.

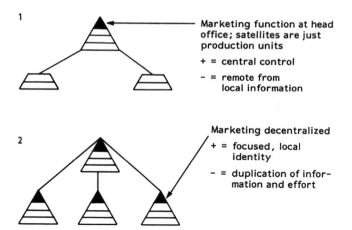

1

Marketing function at head office; satellites are just production units

+ = central control

– = remote from local information

2

Marketing decentralized

+ = focused, local identity

– = duplication of information and effort

Choose an approach where the advantages outweigh the disadvantages.

Try Exercise 11.4

Questions raised for the company

1 Q: What influences whether research is carried out internally or by external consultants?
   A: There can be a number of factors – speed, timing, cost, nature of the research problem, skill requirements, the need for anonymity or objectivity, access of information, etc. Each decision must be taken on its merits.

2 Q: What criteria should be used to assess external researchers?
   A: Again, there are a number of issues to consider.

   (*a*) *Reputation* – in general, in the industry, for particular types of research, etc.

   (*b*) *Capability and experience* – how long established, quality and qualifications of staff, number of staff, repeat business, recommendations and references, etc.

   (*c*) *Organization* – size, links with sources of information, premises, location, geographical coverage, full-time or part-time interviewers, terms of business, etc.

Introduction

To find, maintain or develop a position in any market, depends on having the right information about what is happening in that market. Without having a sensible input of information, the company's decision-making processes will always be suspect.

However, collecting and storing information can be both difficult and costly. Moreover, in times of rapid change, information only has a limited 'shelf life'. Generally speaking, companies have an abundance of information at their disposal, either in their own records or from easily accessed external sources such as trade associations and government departments.

Yet in some ways having too much information can be just as bad as having too little. It becomes difficult to see the wood for the trees. What is required is to cut through what is merely interesting and home in on the information which is necessary, then ensure that it is presented in a usable form.

Exercise 11.1 will investigate just how much marketing information is needed in your company. In addition, it looks at how to get it to the right people, at the right time, in the most appropriate form.

Exercise 11.2 examines the information-gathering techniques at your disposal, their strengths and weaknesses and how you might select one which best meets your requirements.

Exercise 11.3 looks at forecasting in a generalized way so that any confusion about macro versus micro forecasting, and qualitative versus quantitative approaches, can be dispelled.

Exercise 11.4 provides ideas about setting up the right marketing organization.

Exercise 11.1 The marketing information system

Because all companies are in some ways unique, it follows that there are no easy, 'off-the-shelf', marketing information systems available. Even if they were to exist, the chances would be that they would not work. Instead, the company must assemble its own system, and it must be as simple or as sophisticated as the needs of the situation and the budget allows.

The starting point for any system must be to assess the company's information requirements.

INFORMATION REQUIREMENTS

Already, previous work in this book, and the knowledge you have about your company, will suggest certain information requirements to you. However, to ensure that the whole range of possible information requirements is examined, turn to Worksheet 1 which follows and complete it by following the instructions given.

CURRENT INFORMATION SYSTEM

The first worksheet will have highlighted the total information requirements for your company. Put this to one side for the moment and now concentrate on your current system.

Turn to Worksheet 2, and follow the instructions.

PROPOSAL FOR A NEW SYSTEM

Compare the information you gathered in Worksheet 1 and that collected in Worksheet 2. Make a note of the following:

1 Information required but not covered by the current system.
2 Areas of information in the current system that are redundant.
3 Those areas of information that would be more effective if:

   (a) they were presented differently,

(*b*) they were directed to different people,

(*c*) they were provided more or less frequently.

4 From the above analysis make recommendations about how your company's marketing information system might be improved. See Worksheet 3.

Personal notes

WORKSHEET 1 Information requirements (Ex. 11.1)

Below is a list of the areas of business that marketing research could be expected to cover. It doesn't follow that you will need information in all of these areas, but in the light of your earlier study, *tick those that are relevant.*

Then, in the space provided, specify the nature of the information that would be required.

Areas of business	Relevant	Specific information required
Market size		
Market structure		
Market trends		
Market potential		
Market share		
Company communications		
Company image		
Company structure		
Promotion		
Personal selling		
Distribution channels		
Physical distribution		
Packaging		
Profit		
Costs		
Pricing		
Services		
Market research		
Exporting		
New products		
Technical developments		
Competitor activity		
Competitor prices		
Competitor processes		
Competitor products		
Competitor services		

Worksheet 1 (cont'd)

Areas of business	Relevant	Specific information required
User attitude/ behaviour		
Governmental factors		
Economic factors		
Demographic factors		
Add your own areas of business		

WORKSHEET 2 Current information system (Ex. 11.1)

Consider your existing marketing information system and list the various input data, who uses them, for what purpose, the frequency of use and a judgment about whether or not the data are essential, useful or no longer required.

The form below is designed to help you record your findings.

Note: Remember that journals and magazines can be sources of input data just as much as salespeoples' reports and internal control information. You could find it enlightening to include these in your study.

Data input	Used by	Purpose	Frequency	Essential E Useful U Not req. X

Worksheet 2 (cont'd)

Data input	Used by	Purpose	Frequency	Essential E Useful U Not req. X

WORKSHEET 3   Proposal for a new system (Ex.11.1)

Exercise 11.2   Information-gathering techniques

In this exercise you will make a comparative study of various information-gathering techniques and then decide which ones are best suited to solve the company's information requirements.

Step 1   Study Table 11.1 'Information-gathering techniques', and *only proceed to Step 2 when you have read it carefully*.

Step 2   Consider the information gaps you identified in Exercise 11.1 and decide which type of information-gathering technique will be best suited to provide the missing information. In arriving at your answers, you will have to take into account the level of skill in your company and the likely cost.

Exercise 11.3 will also help you in your choice of information-gathering techniques.

If there were no information gaps as a result of completing Exercise 11.1, then review the current information-gathering techniques used in your company and decide if they could be improved upon.

Personal notes

Table 11.1   Information-gathering techniques

Technique	*Main strengths*	*Drawbacks*
Desk research	Can provide quick results, relatively cheap, controllable.	Info. might not be specific enough – interpretation problems. Info. can be out of date.
Company sales records	Readily accessible.	Might not be in a form that can easily be interpreted – mainly historical data.
Company financial records	Readily accessible.	Might not be easily translated into the required form. Mainly historical data.

Table 11.1 Information-gathering techniques

Technique	Main strengths	Drawbacks
Salespersons' reports	Readily accessible current recent info. about customers.	Interpreting narrative into quantified info. can be difficult. Inadequate records.
Journals, etc.	Relatively easy to obtain – libraries, etc.	Info. is not exactly what is required, e.g. too general.
Trade assocs.	Have good understanding of specific trade or industry.	Quality of info. and degree of cooperation from TAs is variable.
Govt. agencies and/or statistics	Vast amount of info., relatively easy access.	Need to know way through govt. systems. Can be swamped with useless information.
External research	Based on competitive environment – will be current information. Provides confidence for decision-making.	Can be costly/time consuming, samples must be accurate – can be difficult to organize.
Questionnaires, face to face	Questioner ensures questions are interpreted correctly – reactions can be noted.	Time-consuming. Can ask loaded questions. Poor design can give rise to misleading results. Costly. Needs skilled interviewer.
Questionnaires, postal	Reach wide audience, relatively cheap.	Failure to get replies back on time (or at all). Filled in by wrong person. Misinterpretation.
Questionnaires, telephone	Instantaneous response, relatively cheap. Do not take up too much of client's time.	Have to be kept brief and so points can be missed. Person gives on the spot information which might be inaccurate.
Depth interviews	Can get to feelings level about products or services. Good qualitative info.	Needs skilled interviewer. Results can be hard to quantify.
Experimentation	Can provide 'actual' customer reaction under test conditions.	Can be expensive. Customer samples must be chosen accurately.
Retail audits	Good quantitive info. about stock movement.	Doesn't explain reasons for stock movements.
Consumer panels	Help to establish patterns of purchases and consumption over a period of time.	Consumers have to be kept motivated to record activities, etc.
Use MR consultants	Doesn't use up staff time. Can produce results in easily digestible form.	Can be costly. How do you choose the right consultants?

Add any other techniques with which you are familiar and list their strengths and drawbacks.

Exercise 11.3   Forecasting techniques

There have been many long and heated debates about whether forecasting is a science or an art. The short answer is that it is a bit of both.

If you were asked to forecast what you will be doing in 2 minutes' time, the chances are you would make a very accurate prediction. The reason for this is obvious, as not very much is going to change in such a short time. Extend the period to tomorrow, next week, a month's time, next year, and your forecasting task would become increasingly difficult.

Companies are forced to look well ahead in order to plan their investment, launch new products and so on. Hence their forecasting task is inherently difficult, unless they operate in some backwater unaffected by mainstream change.

The information they require is sometimes very specific (quantitative) and sometimes fairly general (qualitative). Equally, they need to know what is happening in clearly defined areas of their business (micro forecasting) and sometimes what is happening to total markets (macro forecasting). These aspects of forecasting can be combined, as in the Figure 11.1.

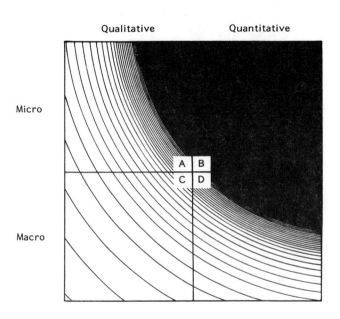

The shading indicates the degree of accuracy that can be expected from the various combinations. Thus the top right-hand corner, quadrant B, demands high accuracy, and calls for scientific rigour, whereas the bottom left-hand corner, quadrant C, relies more on feel, intuition and experience.

Collecting information on which to base a forecast can be a costly business; therefore it is important to recognize the nature of the forecasting problem with which one is faced before setting out. It is pointless to measure something to three decimal places if only a rough and ready measurement is required.

Here is a list of 'forecasting problems'. Referring to Figure 11.1, identify whether the nature of each problem is qualitative, quantitative, micro or macro, i.e. falls in quadrants A, B, C or D. Write the appropriate letter in the space provided.

1   What percentage change (in volume) is expected in the ice-cream market in 2 years' time?   _____

2   What changes in leisure activity are forecast in 5 years' time?   _____

3   What percentage increase in total sales can we expect in our key market segment over the next 12 months?   _____

4   What would the buyers of our X range want to see as product improvements when we remodel the range next year?   _____

5   What changes are expected in our key technology over the next 5 years?   _____

6   In what ways will the voting habits of the UK electorate change by the turn of the century?   _____

7   How many car-users can be expected to be travelling abroad with their vehicles next summer?   _____

8   How many shoppers spending £100 or more can we expect over the next year in our Easthampton store?   _____

The answers are as follows:

1   D
2   C
3   B
4   A
5   A
6   C
7   D
8   B

As a general rule, the margin of error has to be minimal in quadrant B, whereas it is least critical in quadrant C. This clearly has implications for the techniques that are used and the cost of assembling the information.

Look at Exercise 11.2 – 'Information-gathering techniques'.

Exercise 11.4
Organizational structure

Business environments are always changing. Demand patterns change, new technology comes in, new legislation is introduced, there is an economic crisis and so on.

Since the key to successful marketing is to have a suitable organization structure, one that can adjust and cope with the environment, it is not surprising that much experimentation has taken place with the different types of structure. Perhaps no one has yet found the perfect answer to this complex problem of getting the organization right. Nevertheless, research studies have shown that in certain circumstances, some types of structure are going to be more successful than others.

The accompanying worksheet tries to encapsulate these findings in a fairly crude way, showing that structure will to some extent relate to company size and the diversity of its operations. The degree of formality in the marketing planning process will also be related to these factors.

Please answer the following questions:

1 Where would you place your company on the size/complexity of operations continuum?
2 How does your current structure compare with that suggested on the chart?
3 Do the breakdown signals sound familiar?
4 In what ways do you think your structure ought to change?

Personal notes

WORKSHEET   Organizational structure (Ex. 11.4)

Place an x on each of the four lines below to indicate where your
organization lies

Company size   small ————————————————————▶ large

Diversity of   low ————————————————————▶ high
products

Diversity of   low ————————————————————▶ high
markets

Degree of   low ————————————————————▶ high
formalization
of planning

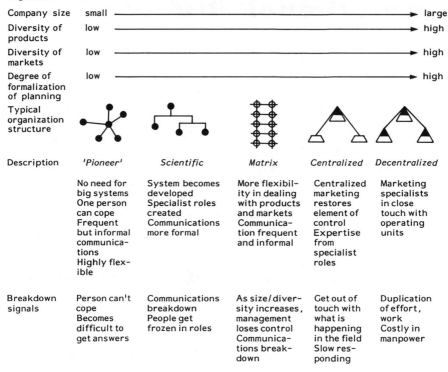

Typical organization structure					
Description	*'Pioneer'*	*Scientific*	*Matrix*	*Centralized*	*Decentralized*
	No need for big systems One person can cope Frequent but informal communications Highly flexible	System becomes developed Specialist roles created Communications more formal	More flexibility in dealing with products and markets Communication frequent and informal	Centralized marketing restores element of control Expertise from specialist roles	Marketing specialists in close touch with operating units
Breakdown signals	Person can't cope Becomes difficult to get answers	Communications breakdown People get frozen in roles	As size/diversity increases, management loses control Communications breakdown	Get out of touch with what is happening in the field Slow responding	Duplication of effort, work Costly in manpower

Figure 11.1

12 Implementing the marketing plan

| Conditions that must be satisfied |

1   Any closed-loop planning system, especially if it is based just on forecasting and budgeting, will deaden any creative response and will eventually lead to failure.
2   Marketing planning which is not integrated with other functional areas of the business at general management level will be largely ineffective.
3   The separation of operational and strategic marketing planning will lead to divergent plans, with the short-term viewpoint winning because it achieves quick results.
4   The chief executive must take an active role.
5   It can take 3 years to introduce marketing planning successfully.

Try Exercises 12.1 and 12.2

| Ten principles of marketing planning |

1   Develop the strategic plan first; the operational plan comes out of this.
2   Put marketing as close as possible to the customer and have marketing and sales under one person.
3   Marketing is an attitude of mind, not a set of procedures.
4   Organize activities around customer groups, not functional activities.
5   A marketing audit must be rigorous. No vague terms should be allowed, and nothing should be hidden. Managers should use tools like portfolio analysis and product life cycle.
6   SWOT analyses should be focused on segments that are critical to the business; concentrate only on key factors which lead to objectives.
7   People must be educated about the planning process.
8   There has to be a plan for planning.
9   All objectives should be prioritized in terms of their urgency and impact.

10 Marketing planning needs the active support of the chief executive and must be appropriate for the culture.

Planning horizon

There is a natural point of focus in the future beyond which it is pointless to plan for. This can differ . n firm to firm, depending on its business. Generally, small firms can use shorter horizons, because they are flexible, to adjust to change. Large firms need longer horizons.

Planning paradox

Companies often set out to achieve the impossible. It is not unknown to see planning objectives which seek to:

● Maximize sales.
● Minimize costs.
● Increase market share.
● Maximize profits.

  Not only are these incompatible, but they damage the credibility of the managers who subscribe to such commitments.

Question raised for the company

Q: Are there different approaches to marketing planning?
A: We believe there are. Please see the diagram below.

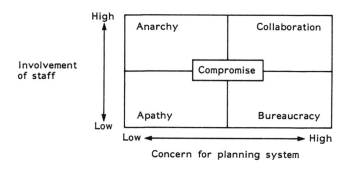

The most successful marketing plans are collaborative. Here, relevant executives take part in the process in a caring way, and at the same time planning is done rigorously.

Introduction

As the brief notes have indicated, there are a number of conditions to be met if the marketing planning process is not to become a sterile, closed-loop system. The ten principles of marketing planning listed in the notes go a considerable way to ensuring that the process does not degenerate into a ritualized, 'numbers game'. However, there are still some problematical issues to be addressed.

Exercise 12.1 looks at the theory issue of how formalized the planning process should be, and how to take the correct steps to get close to the ideal system for your company.

Exercise 12.2 examines how to set up a timetable for planning. This is particularly useful in getting all contributors to the marketing plan working in unison, and coming up with the necessary information at the appropriate time.

In this chapter you will focus on the marketing planning system best suited to your company. By way of consolidating on all of your work through this book, you will design an appropriate planning system and lay down the 'ground rules' for its implementation.

Exercise 12.1 Designing the marketing planning system

SELECTING THE APPROPRIATE APPROACH

Figure 12.1 shows how the degree of formalization of the marketing planning process relates to company size and the diversity of its operations.

1 Select a position on this figure which best describes your company's situation.
2 In the space below, write down a few key words or sentences that would best describe the marketing planning system you would need for your company, e.g. high formalization, etc.

Company size

		Large	Medium	Small
Market/product diversity	High	High formalization	High/medium formalization	Medium formalization
	Medium	High/medium formalization	Medium formalization	Low formalization
	Low	Medium formalization	Low formalization	Very low formalization

Figure 12.1   Marketing planning

IDENTIFYING THE IMPROVEMENT AREAS

1 Imagine that it is possible to measure the efficiency of a marketing planning system on a scale 0–100, where 100 is equivalent to a 100 per cent efficiency, i.e. the system works well and conforms with your model. How would you rate the current approach to marketing planning in your company? To what extent does it match up with your ideal?
2 Enter your score on Figure 12.2, drawing a horizontal line as shown.

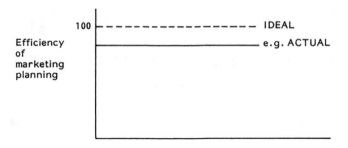

Figure 12.2

The difference between your scoreline and the ideal must represent where there is room for improvement.

Transfer your score line to Worksheet 1, the Force Field Diagram, then complete the worksheet by following the instructions given below.

3   Identify all those factors that have 'pushed' your actual efficiency line below the ideal. Add them to Worksheet 1, showing them as actual forces pushing down. If you can, represent the biggest forces with longer arrows as shown in Figure 12.3. ˙

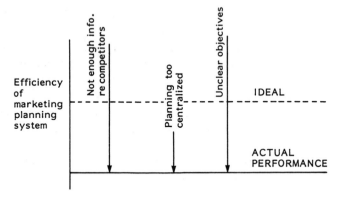

Figure 12.3

You will probably have more than three factors, so list as many as you can. Remember you should be noting only those that affect the *marketing planning system*, not the company's general approach to marketing. We will call these downward forces 'restraining forces', because they are acting against improvement.

4   Now ask yourself why isn't the actual performance line you have drawn lower than it is. The reason is of course that there are

several parts of the system that work well, or there are other strengths in your company. Identify these positive forces and add them to Worksheet 1, as shown in Figure 12.4, again relating the arrow size approximately to the influence of each factor.

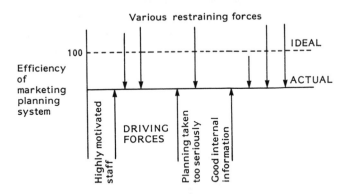

Figure 12.4

Again the factors shown above are only examples. You will identify many more. We call these 'Driving Forces' because they are pushing towards improvement.

5   The worksheet should now be complete, showing the two sets of forces lined up against each other. What next? Well, it might have struck you that what you have assembled is somewhat analogous to a ship at sea. Your ship (the marketing planning system) is wallowing below its ideal level in the water but is prevented from sinking by buoyant forces (driving forces). To restore the ship to its correct level, it would be natural to remove or jettison some of the cargo (the restraining forces), not to try to get out and push from below.

As it is for the ship, so it is for your marketing planning system, therefore:

(a) Select the major restraining forces and work out ways that you can reduce their impact or preferably eliminate them altogether. These will be the source of the greatest improvements, but some remedies might need time to take effect.

(b) So concurrently select minor restraining forces and plan to eliminate them also. Although their impact on improvement might be less, you will probably find they respond more quickly to treatment.

(c) Finally select the smallest driving forces and work out if there are any ways to increase their impact.

6 Assemble your various responses to 5(a), (b) and (c) together into a comprehensive improvement plan, then take steps to get it accepted and acted upon.

Put most of your energy into removing the restraining factors. To focus on the major driving forces, e.g. trying to make highly motivated staff even more motivated, is likely to be counter-productive.

WORKSHEET   Force field diagram (Ex. 12.1)

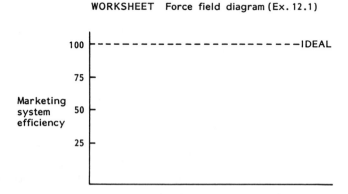

FORCE FIELD ANALYSIS THEORY

The force field analysis upon which much of designing a system is based, stems from the work of Kurt Lewin (*Field Theory in Social Science*, Harper, 1951). His reasoning, adapted to the programme situation, operates thus:

1 If a Company's marketing system is functioning well then the Company could be said to have no problems. Diagrammatically the efficiency level could be shown at something approaching 100 per cent. See Figure 12.5.

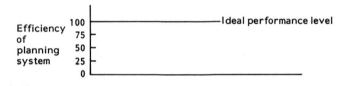

Figure 12.5

2 Few companies reach this happy state of affairs. Without resorting to concise measurement (a consensus of views is generally enough),

most companies would 'score' their planning system somewhat lower, as shown in Figure 12.6.

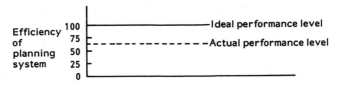

Figure 12.6

3 Wherever the 'actual' line is drawn, it poses two interesting questions upon which the subsequent analysis hinges, namely:

(*a*) What causes the performance level to be where it is?
(*b*) Why doesn't it fall any lower?

4 Clearly the answer to 3(*a*) is that things are going wrong in the system; that there are missing or malfunctioning areas. Until these are put right, there will always be a drag on the efficiency, holding it down. These negative forces are termed *restraining forces* because they are restraining improvement.

5 Similarly, the reason that efficiency doesn't drop lower than has been shown is that there must be several parts of the planning system that work quite well. There are many strengths in the system. These positive factors are termed *driving forces* because they are the forces pushing towards better efficiency.

6 In Figure 12.6, for the efficiency of the planning system to be below the ideal level, then the restraining forces must be greater than the driving forces.

7 Let's take a simple illustration. We are driving a car and it's going more slowly than it ought to because the brakes are rubbing (restraining force). If we want to resume driving at normal speed then we have two courses of action open to us:

(*a*) We can put our foot down on the accelerator (increase the driving force)
(*b*) We can free the brakes (remove the restraining force).

We can see that by putting our foot down all sorts of troubles are likely to materialize. Unless something is done to free the brakes, then probably they would overheat, perhaps catch fire or jam up completely.

8 A similar overheating could take place in the company's marketing

planning system unless it is tackled properly. To get lasting improvements, it will be important to identify all the restraining and driving forces. Indeed much of the earlier work in this study programme was designed to do just this. Using this information it will be important *to plan how to reduce or remove the restraining forces and, only when that is done, consider how to plan to boost the driving forces*.

9 Figure 12.7 is an example of how a finished force field diagram might look, although most people will have identified several more factors than shown here. Many of the factors identified by you ought to be unique to your company.

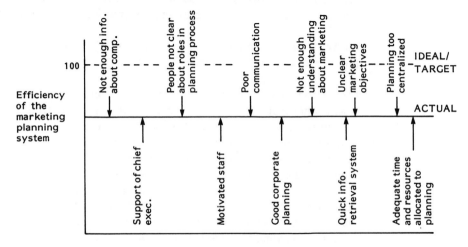

Figure 12.7

Notes

1 Remember that only factors that affect the marketing planning process ought to appear in the force field diagram.

2 It is possible to draw the force arrows proportional in length to their influence.

Exercise 12.2 Implementing the marketing planning system

Perhaps you will be unable to implement a marketing planning system until your improvement plan from Exercise 12.1 has eliminated the more serious obstacles. Nevertheless, from what you have read in this book, you will know that a successful marketing planning system will have to follow these steps.

1 There will have to be guidance provided by the corporate objectives.
2 A marketing audit must take place.
3 A gap analysis completed.
4 A SWOT analysis drawn up.
5 Assumptions and contingencies considered.
6 Marketing objectives and strategies set.
7 Individual marketing programmes established.
8 A period of review and measurement.

Because of the work required, all this takes time. Various people might have to participate at different stages. There will certainly have to be several meetings or discussions with other functional departments, either to get information or to ensure collaboration.

Therefore, in order to keep the planning 'train' on the 'rails', it will be in everybody's interest to be clear about the sequencing of these different activities, to have a schedule or timetable.

As the company gets more experienced in planning, then probably the timetable can be tightened up and the whole planning period shortened. However, to get events into perspective, it is often helpful to present a timetable of the planning activities, as shown in Figure 12.8. The circle represents a calendar year and the time periods are merely examples – not to be taken as recommended periods.

In the second planning year, months 11 and 12 could be used to evaluate the first year's plan and thereby prepare information for the next round of corporate planning.

This diagrammatic approach clearly shows how the planning process is a continual undercurrent throughout the year.

Now, as your final task try drawing up the planning timetable for your company on Figure 12.9.

Figure 12.8

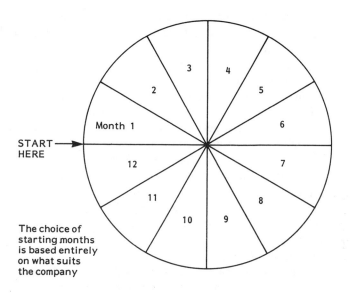

Figure 12.9

Index

Index

**SENIOR PARTNER IN A
FIRM OF SOLICITORS**

SCHOOL TEACHER

GROUP CHAIRMAN

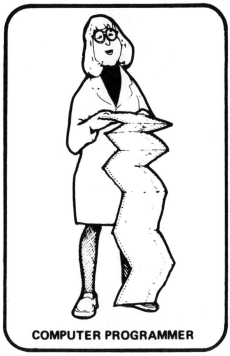

COMPUTER PROGRAMMER

LIFT ATTENDANT

LOCAL BANK MANAGER

BRICKLAYER

TOOL-MAKER

MACHINE OPERATOR

ELDERLY GRANNIE

SALES MANAGER

SELF-EMPLOYED PLUMBER

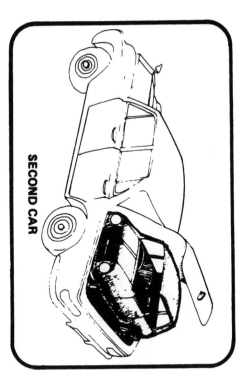

SECOND CAR

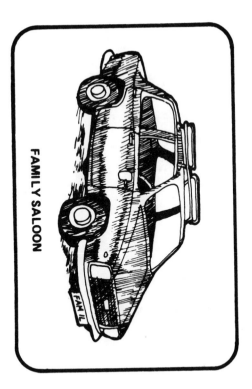

FAMILY SALOON

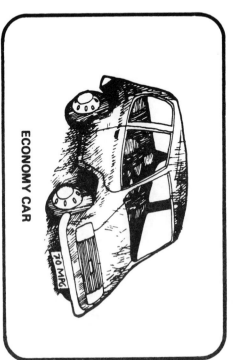

ECONOMY CAR

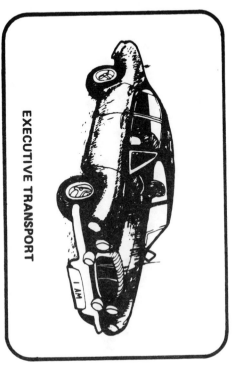

EXECUTIVE TRANSPORT

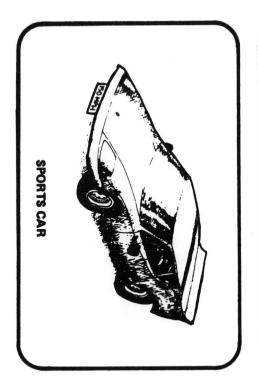

SPORTS CAR

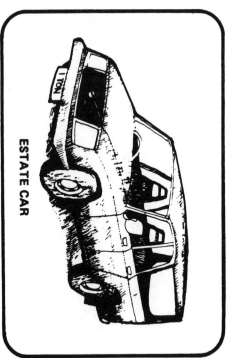

ESTATE CAR